MAKING A LASTING DIFFERENCE

MAKING A LASTING DIFFERENCE

Sustaining non-profit organisations and their impact

Graeme Reekie

Making a Lasting Difference: Sustaining non-profit organisations and their impact

Visit our websites at www.WrenandGreyhound.co.uk and www.TheLastingDifference.com

First Printing: April 2019
Wren and Greyhound Limited

ISBN 978-0-9541506-5-5

ACKNOWLEDGEMENTS

The ideas in this book have been developed and tested in my company's consultancy with large and small organisations in every sector of the non-profit world since 2012. The concepts have helped us mentor and support leaders as they find their way through strategic and financial upheaval. Our understanding has been deepened by the responses, questions and challenges that countless people have generously shared in workshops, seminars, conference presentations, action learning sets, board away days, senior management team meetings and our leadership retreats. Directly or indirectly this book is the work of thousands of people.

Thank you to my colleagues Jen Curran, Laura Lebec, Debbie Bayne and Caspia Baird for all manner of help in bringing the book to the world. Special thanks to my 'beta readers' Norma Norris, Lorna Ascroft, Sue Beer, Jacquie Winning, Joyce Duncan and proofer Jackie Borge for invaluable support in getting over the finishing line. Thanks to John Miers for Wren and Greyhound's visual language. Thanks also to Carol Downie for reminding me of 'the second curve', Bridie Ashrowan for getting me started on ecosystems and Elaine Wilson for suggesting a systems aspect to defining sustainability. The sections on system-level interventions were crowd-sourced and tested at a conference on Preventing Market Failure run by the Coalition of Care and Support Providers Scotland (CCPS) - special thanks to Dee Fraser for this and countless other opportunities and insights over the years. To Jess Wade, Anne-Marie Monaghan, Moxie DePaulitte, Claire Cairns and Paddy Carstairs for inspiration on involvement; Virginia Anderson, Flora Henderson, Isobel Lawson, Deanna Wolf, Catriona Henderson, Sasha Taylor and Frances Simpson for enthusiastic advocacy and sustained support. To all the Think Tank and learning set members who helped test my ideas over the years, thank you.

To the partners with whom some of the book's ideas first took shape: The Association for Chief Officers of Scottish Voluntary Organisations, Association for Real Change, Children England, Corra Foundation, Coalition of Care and Support Providers in Scotland, Dundee Carers Centre, Evaluation Support Scotland, The Funders' Forum, Impact Funding Partners, The Institute of Fundraising, LGBT Youth Scotland, MECOPP, Paths for All, Penumbra, Quality Scotland, Robertson Trust, Scotland's International Development Alliance, Scottish Government, Shared Care Scotland, WWF. Extra special thanks to those organisations and individuals who have shared their feedback and resources via www.TheLastingDifference.com.

Dedicated to Wren and a rather special otter, without whom...

CONTENTS

FOREWORD

Ask the manager, staff or funder of any non-profit organisation their biggest concern and they'll tell you it's sustainability. They will talk about shrinking finances, increasing demand, limited capacity, managing growth.

But it's not all about organisations. One of the reasons I came to research and write about sustainability is that more and more clients were coming to me with briefs that sounded a lot like 'Can you help us survive?'. In those days, all I could offer them were challenging questions like, 'What right do you have to survive?' and 'Who would notice if you were gone?'.

A core theme of this book is that organisations don't have an inherent or self-evident right to exist. But it bothered me that I didn't have a good answer to the question of sustainability. What does it mean? What would it look like? Would we recognise it if we saw it? And why was everyone talking about something without knowing what it means? Had anyone even attempted to define sustainability in this context?

Fast-forward five years and I think we can start to answer these questions. This book is based on the learning I have generated with many hundreds of organisations since starting to explore the subject deeply and directly in 2013. Thousands more have used and commented on the popular 'Lasting Difference' toolkit, which this book also draws and expands upon. Although it's informed by lots of reading and research, it's thoroughly and unashamedly grounded in practice. There are useful theories, concepts and models in here, but they are pointless if they don't help organisations and managers with their everyday challenges.

The most pleasing feedback I get is when people tell me the ideas are simple, but that they have depth behind them. I hope you find this a simple, useful and useable book and that it supports you to think deeply and in new ways about today's most pressing concerns.

Graeme Reekie

PART 1: UNDERSTANDING NON-PROFIT SUSTAINABILITY

CHAPTER 1: INTRODUCTION

Where are we and how did we get here?

In some ways, the non-profit world is healthier than ever. In terms of the number of organisations, revenue and size of workforce, the sector has grown throughout the economic turmoil of the years since the 2008 financial crisis. In fact, one of the things that gives people the heart to face today's sustainability challenges is knowing they've survived previous ones.

However, there are very real and legitimate concerns about the future of individual organisations and the sector as a whole. Much of the sector's growth has come from larger organisations. Most of these are providers of health and social care services, a sector which has become increasingly reliant on public service contracts. This at a time when public sector finances are under immense pressure, leading to lower budgets, higher levels of demand and increased competition for resources. At the same time, new policy and regulatory expectations, valuable as they are, increase costs (for example, employee rights to a 'living wage' and payment for sleepover shifts in the UK, and overtime payments in the US).

These challenges put unsustainable strains on sector and organisational capacity and the cracks are showing. Public trust in charities is falling. Many organisations are becoming insolvent. In some cases, this might be a technical insolvency, for example where pension deficits outweigh assets, or where reserves are insufficient to cover short-term operating costs. But it is increasingly common to find organisations drawing on reserves to supplement income, boards approving deficit budgets, or having to make tough choices about reducing services or staffing. In my own recent practice, there was one month in which I was supporting the survival of a charity while *in the same city* three more organisations *in the same sector* were appealing for emergency bail-out monies.

There is a sustainability problem in our sector and it's not going away any time soon.

Where we're going
This book aims to:

- Make it easier for people in organisations to make sense of, assess, prioritise and take action on sustainability.
- Create a shared framework and language for discussing the subject.
- Provide practical tools to help non-profit organisations make a lasting difference into the future.

How we'll get there
We can't solve problems by using the same thinking that created them. For that reason, I would encourage the reader to be suspicious of expert, top-down, rational advice and simple answers, including any that you find in this book. My professional education is as a trainer and manager. The things I learned on my MBA changed the way I think, work and live. Many of the ideas in this book have parallels in or draw on mainstream management theory (see the References section for specifics). But I am suspicious of managerialism because planning, objectives and experts can only get us so far. The book encourages a more systemic approach, encouraging us to address not just the cognitive aspects and impacts of sustainability, but the social and emotional aspects too.

Put simply, for your organisation's work to survive, other people need to care about whether it does or not.

As we will see, sustainability is a hugely complex topic about working in hugely complex environments. Some of the ideas in this book will be familiar to you. Others will be new. They are all designed to help you think about and tackle familiar problems in new ways, but there are no easy answers. So, as you work through the book, be critical and ask yourself 'Do I recognise this reality?', 'Can this idea help me?', and most importantly, 'How can I test this out for myself?'.

Note on language

This book uses the words 'non-profit' 'organisations' and their 'funders'.

Non-profit

In this context, 'non-profit' is used in preference to 'voluntary organisation' or 'charity' for several reasons:

- It is broad enough to include social enterprises (organisations that trade to reinvest profit in social impact), but less jargonistic than 'third sector'
- It can be taken to include public sector organisations (in the UK this includes schools, hospitals, governing bodies, regulators etc.)
- It is shorter and less clunky than the more common 'not-for-profit'
- It is recognisable to non-UK audiences
- Most voluntary organisations are staffed by paid professionals, retaining voluntarism only at board or grassroots level.

Organisations

Referring to 'organisations' might be frustrating for readers who manage 'projects' or 'services' within larger organisations over which they may have little influence. The book is primarily aimed at organisational leaders, but most of its content will be just as relevant at a project or service level, often just by substituting the word 'project' for 'organisation'. I use 'project' to describe time-limited pieces of work set up (and usually funded) for a particular purpose and period of time. 'Services' tend to last beyond single funding cycles, as they are the way organisations structure core activities.

Trustees

I will refer to 'trustees' not 'directors' or 'committee members'. This is because not all non-profits are also registered companies (where trustees are also company directors), and because senior managers are also often called 'directors'. For clarity, when I refer to trustees, I mean the unpaid members of an organisation's board (or management committee, e.g. if the organisation is not formally constituted as a charity or company).

Funders

I generally refer to the people and organisations who give money to non-profit organisations as 'funders' rather than 'donors', 'commissioners', or 'customers'. Although 'funder' is commonly used to describe providers of grants, it has a broader meaning than the other words, which I use in the following ways:

'Donor' – typically a member of the public who gives their own money. Amounts might be large or small, given freely or with some expectations.

'Commissioner' – someone who works for a local or national government body and purchases services on a contractual basis.

'Customers' – are people or organisations that non-profits trade with, exchanging goods or services for a payment or return of some kind. Although it is a broader term than 'funder', it can provoke strong reactions from people who do not believe non-profits either do or should operate in a 'market'. At the same time, thinking of all of the above stakeholders as 'customers' can be a very valuable exercise. What do people want in return for the money they give you? (And if you don't know, how can you find out?).

While we're at it, I define stakeholders as people or organisations who can affect or *be affected by* an organisation's work.

CHAPTER 2: ABOUT NON-PROFIT SUSTAINABILITY

Sustainability is the word we use to talk about organisational resilience and survival. It may be the wrong word to use, because of its connection with 'green' or environmental issues. Indeed, the word has several meanings and uses. These are explored below to help us understand what sustainability is not, and what it might be, before arriving at a new definition of what it is.

At its most simple, sustainability describes a situation where resources are replenished at least as quickly as they are used. Imagine a bath of water with the plug taken out but with the taps still running. As long as the taps are adding at least the same amount of water as the drain takes away, the water level will be sustained.

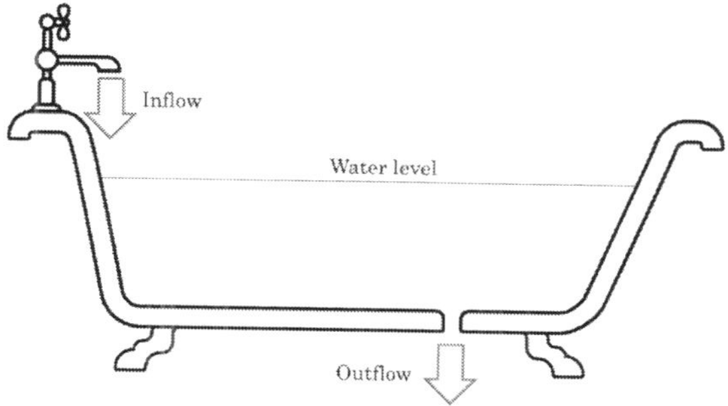

Figure 1: Sustainability means being able to replenish resources more quickly than they are used.

The mistake many people make when applying this to organisations is to think that money is the only resource that makes an organisation sustainable – or the most important one. Of course, money is important. But so are clients, supporters, staffing, knowledge, time, reliable supplies, safe equipment etc.

We might also think that sustainability means keeping the water level constant. And, as we shall see, capacity is a fundamentally important element of sustainability. But, however desirable it can seem when we are in the midst of chaos, equilibrium is a sign of stasis, and stasis is the enemy of sustainability. Organisational sustainability requires constant adjustment of inflows, outflows and capacity. It therefore requires interaction with the environment – but it shouldn't be confused with environmental sustainability – see below.

What it's not

It's not about the environment and being 'green'
Although the potential for the word to be confused with environmental issues is sometimes unhelpful, environmental ideas and metaphors are actually very relevant:

What's going on in your organisation's external environment?
What sort of environment is it? A garden? A jungle? A desert?
What is your organisation's internal ecosystem like?
What stage is it at in its lifecycle?

I'm writing this on a sunny day, looking out over my garden to the greenhouse. The tomato plants enjoy the heat and are growing well this year. But if I don't water them they'll die in just a few days.

This is like the organisation in Figure 2. It perceives itself to be in a closed system like my greenhouse. Only people within the organisation contribute to it. Things are kept in-house. The organisation believes itself to be self-reliant, in control of its destiny. Safe.

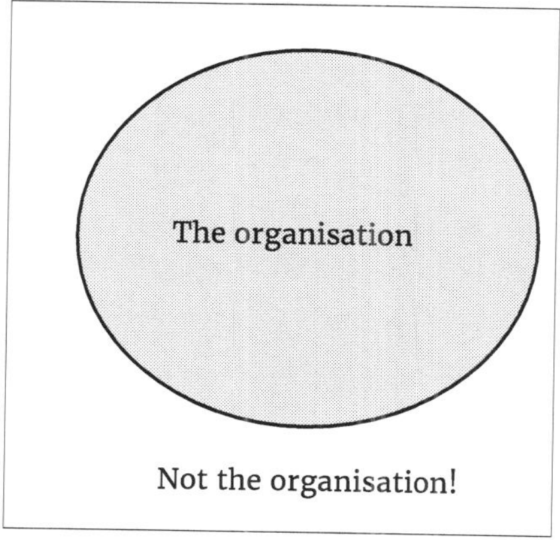

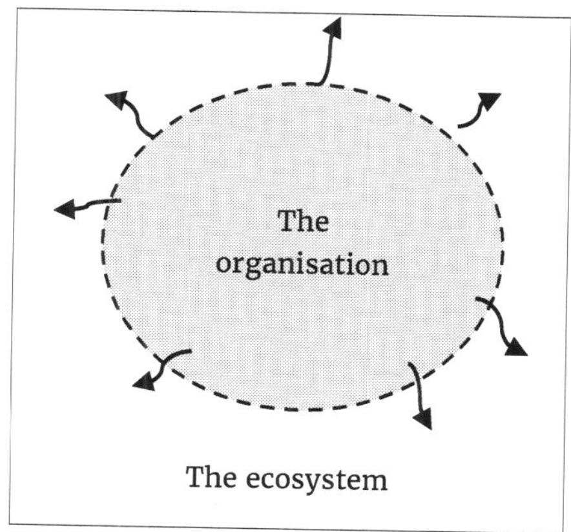

Figure 2: The organisation as a closed system
Figure 3: The sustainable organisation, part of a healthy ecosystem

Although this is sounds exaggerated, it's how organisations commonly approach sustainability. How can they find the resources they need to survive? How can they sustain themselves? Can they shelter from external forces? Now imagine that instead of writing this, I go and take the roof off the greenhouse, exposing the tomato plants. On the downside, they'll be colder at night. But on the up-side this should make them hardier and less prone to disease. And crucially, they'll be watered by the rain. They can survive without me. Their fruit will eventually ripen, fall and rot, releasing and nourishing seeds for next year. Birds and animals might even eat the fruit and spread the seeds elsewhere. The tomatoes have a better chance of a sustainable future as part of an open ecosystem.

The organisation in Figure 3 is part of an ecosystem, exchanging things with its environment. Organisational boundaries are permeable, allowing ideas, intelligence, people and resources to flow across them. This nourishes and replenishes the organisation's resources. It encourages change and growth, building resilience in response to a changing environment. Of course, this will mean letting some things go too. When times are tight, Organisation A is likely to clench up, ceasing investment and making false economies like reducing training budgets, pulling out of partnership meetings, not allowing staff to take part in conferences and events etc. It may focus so much on protecting its ideas and resources that it forgets to give anything back.

Reflection:
Of the two organisations, which has a better chance of a sustainable future?

To what extent does this depend on the ecosystem in which they find themselves?

Sustainability is not about organisational stability – or survival
Sometimes people talk about sustainability in terms of organisational survival. But sustainability isn't just about survival. Things change. And things end. This is very important – your organisation won't survive by staying the same. It *has* to *evolve*. If it focuses on survival for its own sake it won't survive. This is the first paradox of sustainability, one we'll explore in more detail in Chapter 3.

It's more than just financial viability
Many people think that financial viability is what sustainability really amounts to: if organisations earn more than they spend, they're sustainable. Where non-profit sustainability resources and workshops exist, this is where they tend to put their emphasis. And healthy finances are a crucial part of sustainability. But they don't exist in a vacuum.

For instance, it's easy to think of organisations which have been financially healthy, but which have not survived because of poor management, incompetent governance, ineffective practices, untrained staff, poor customer service, lack of adaptability, antagonistic stakeholder relationships - and so on. Money is important, but it's not enough. Finance and funding need to be understood as part of a holistic approach to organisational sustainability.

It's easy to think of organisations which have been financially healthy, but which have not survived because they were badly run, their staff were unhappy, they ignored their customers or they didn't adapt, innovate or change.

It's not about sustainable competitive advantage

If sustainability is mentioned in traditional management literature, the focus is typically on 'sustainable competitive advantage'. The short answer: organisations must protect and exploit their resources before someone else does. There's a lot to be said for that definition, but it is again too narrow. It doesn't really fit a sector that is characterised by values, openness and involvement, even if the non-profit world is more competitive than ever.

There is also a good deal of literature on environmental sustainability, which is starting to broaden to include the social impact of commercial activities, for example within Corporate Social Responsibility. The recently developed approach known as 'Shared Value' is closer to the definition of true sustainability, with its interest in cross-sector investment, multi-agency partnerships and social impact. But until it becomes their raison d'être (rather than enlightened self-interest) commercial businesses and management theory are more likely to be interested in the 'competitive advantage' definition of sustainability.

What it might be

Sustainable impact – making a lasting difference

We need to be honest. Despite the reasons many people will have for reading this book, sustainability is not all about organisations. What right does your organisation have to exist? Who does it serve? Who does it matter to? What difference does it make?

Sometimes sustainability is about equipping people, ideas or issues not to need us anymore - building the capacity of people, communities, even other organisations, to sustain things for themselves or carry on our work and messages without us. A useful definition of sustainability has to include the reason non-profits exist: to make a difference.

A new definition

For all of the reasons above, and for more that are explored below, non-profit sustainability can be defined as:

The capacity of an organisation, service or system to make a lasting difference.

There is a lot of meaning in this simple statement. 'Capacity' reflects the notions above about finance, resource renewal and healthy organisational cultures. The inclusion of 'systems' is important to note. An organisation might do everything right and still not be sustainable if it finds itself in a particularly hostile funding or policy environment. The 'lasting difference' part of the definition reflects the importance of non-profit organisations making a positive impact on the people and causes they serve. As we have noted, it is not all about organisations. Nevertheless, this book aims to help organisations ensure they have done everything they can to anticipate and withstand these forces.

PART 2: THE PARADOXES OF SUSTAINABILITY

CHAPTER 3: INTRODUCING THE PARADOXES, PRINCIPLES AND PRACTICES OF SUSTAINABILITY

There are good reasons why sustainability is the number one issue for non-profit organisations and their funders. But it's too simple to say that sustainability challenges arise because there is more competition for fewer resources. If this was the only challenge, there would be fairly straightforward solutions to it. The situation is much more complicated than resource scarcity. Sustainability traps us in a bind because it requires us to balance competing priorities, reconcile different pressures, meet conflicting stakeholder expectations, and make difficult trade-off decisions.

This chapter presents these challenges as four complex paradoxes and a myth, each with some principles which are both easy to believe and hard to live up to. However, the principles help us to understand sustainability and manage the paradoxes better. Each set of paradoxes and principles is therefore followed by a few straightforward practices. Part 3 presents many more of these alongside each of the five capabilities of sustainable organisations.

None of the paradoxes that follow are intended to be judgmental. They are inevitable consequences of the way things work in the non-profit world and most organisations grapple with them in one way or another. They are summarised here then explored in more depth in separate chapters below.

The Change Paradox
The first paradox is that it is only by changing that organisations can be sustainable. If we stay the same while the world around us is evolving, we'll be left behind. Our work will become irrelevant to people and communities whose needs, aspirations and abilities are also changing.

The Octopus Paradox
This paradox arises because of the Change Paradox. When we need to change to survive, we need to reach out in new directions and sense new opportunities. The paradox is that diversifying income by diversifying activity can increase risk.

The Yes/No Paradox
To be healthy, organisations need funding, partnerships, referrals and new developments. But many sustainability challenges actually arise *because* organisations have said 'yes' to too many of these things in the hope that this will make them sustainable. The things that organisations need to survive can also kill them. Sustainability requires organisations to know when and how to say 'no'.

The Efficiency Paradox
The fourth and final paradox is that, without efficiency, organisations would quickly exhaust all of their energy and resources; but too much of it means they won't have the capacity to develop. They can't innovate, be responsive – be sustainable.

The Myth of Perpetual Motion
Most commonly, this is the mistaken belief that organisations can keep going once funding stops. The myth is also prevalent in strategic planning and organisational change initiatives when momentum is expected to be sustained without continued input. There is a reason the perpetual motion machine has not been invented. Nothing in the known universe is self-sustaining.

CHAPTER 4: THE CHANGE PARADOX

The Change Paradox: Only by changing can organisations be sustainable.

The principle here is that sustainability does not mean 'sustained'. When discussing sustainability, it's important to be clear that we are not arguing for maintaining the status quo or being resistant to learning and change. Quite the opposite - non-profit organisations usually exist to change the status quo. And learning, like capacity, is absolutely core to sustainability.

One of the key themes of this book is that organisations need to continually learn and adapt. Equally, few funders fund activities, or even outcomes, for their own sake these days. Whether they call it this or not (and most don't, yet), the trend is towards funding being a form of action research, investing in projects to generate learning about unmet needs and how they can be most effectively addressed. Sustainability requires learning and change, not maintenance and stasis. In a changing world, the only certainty is that organisations that don't adapt will fail.

Talking about sustainability can also sound like organisations are primarily interested in their own survival. This is dangerous because non-profit organisations exist to serve a purpose other than their own existence. Sustainability is not about keeping things going. Nowhere in an organisation's constitution or founding documents does it say the organisation exists for its own sake, or to pay people's wages. It might not even be desirable or necessary for an organisation's work to continue. Many non-profits exist to build capacity so that other people, communities or organisations can provide for themselves. If they don't withdraw from some projects or areas of work,

they won't have the capacity to reach new ones. And they'll just create dependency. So, sustainability is also about making a sustainable impact, for example leaving a legacy where a project's work or messages can carry on without it.
Keeping organisations going, keeping people in a job, or making sure projects are funded might all be important. But if organisations pursue them for their own sake they will, paradoxically but almost certainly, become unsustainable.

It is counterproductive for organisations to focus on sustaining their work because:

It pulls them off course, causing mission-drift (see the Octopus Paradox).
They lose their identity, focus and purpose.
They try to become all things to all people.
Capacity gets stretched to breaking point as organisations do more work in more areas, each with different funding and reporting requirements.
Organisations adopt unsustainable competitive practices, e.g. underpricing their work to win financially unsustainable contracts.
It encourages dependency and the belief that people (or messages and campaigns) can't survive without support.
It's commercially naïve: funders and supporters have a keen nose for organisations that are simply chasing the money.

In the non-profit world, organisations exist to pursue a mission. Their job should be to do themselves out of a job. Although it's common for organisations to say this, it's much harder to live up to, particularly for boards and managers who commonly feel the responsibility of sustaining staffing, projects and the organisation above all else. However, sustainable organisations focus on their goals, not survival; they seek funding that aligns with their strategies. Unsustainable organisations follow the money. This leads to the Octopus Paradox, the second of our four Paradoxes. Before introducing the Octopus, we will summarise the Change Paradox and suggest some practices that can help to reconcile and manage it.

Overview – the Paradox in brief

The Change Paradox: Only by changing can organisations be sustained.

Principle: Sustainability does not mean 'sustained'.

Practice: Learn, adapt and evolve purposefully.

The paradox in practice
In the sections that follow, suggested practices are presented at a number of different levels:

- **System-level:** for funders, policy makers and others who have a role in shaping a sustainable ecosystem in which non-profit organisations exist.
- **Board level:** for trustees and directors but also senior leaders who take part in board discussions and decisions.
- **Management level:** for Chief Officers and managers at different levels in an organisation.
- **Operational level:** for staff at different levels, which might include some managers.

As will be seen, there is a good deal of crossover between the different levels of practice, so regardless of your role you should find relevant ideas in every section.

System-level responses to the Change Paradox

People with an interest in a sustainable non-profit sector can help shape the environment by thinking (and communicating) clearly about sustainability in the context of *adaptation, evolution* and *change*. To support change, learning needs to be prioritised at the system level.

- **Prioritise and encourage system learning**

For policy makers (and policy organisations), developing policy and having it approved and adopted is a significant undertaking, often taking many years of hard work, research and influencing. Policy is a potentially powerful lever for system change.

But systems and societies are complex and not usually amenable to being changed by one lever alone. Successful policy and strategy implementation is the key. This is where policy makers need to enlist the help of others in *learning*, as they are unlikely to know the best ways for the policy to be implemented or have the resources to do so.

Of course, system leaders must have the confidence to acknowledge that they don't have all the answers. They need to be open to learning and use their resources to facilitate it.

Case study – Scottish Government Community Safety

In 2012, the Scottish Government planned to address intra-Christian sectarianism, a complex and politically sensitive topic. It tasked a short-life expert advisory group of academics, faith leaders and other non-profit leaders to inform policy based on evidence and definitions that were specific to Scotland. Alongside this, it developed a time-limited fund to support community activity to understand the effectiveness of interventions.

What was particularly interesting was that neither the need nor the outcomes were assumed at the outset. The fund explicitly set out to explore the ways sectarianism was perceived, understood and impacted in communities, and the extent to which it was a priority to them. These learning goals were the fund's main outcomes. Organisations which received funding were therefore not just required to undertake activities and measure their effectiveness, like they would be in any fund. They were explicitly tasked with generating evidence. The only outcomes they were required to work towards were the learning outcomes. Nevertheless, a group of organisations came together with the support of the fund administrators (Voluntary Action Fund) to develop an outcome framework and evaluation guide to help shape the learning.

The politicians and civil servants who selected this approach bravely acknowledged the limitations of their knowledge of the issue and of their power to address it alone. By actively involving non-profit organisations in generating learning, they and the Advisory Group were rewarded with good quality evidence to inform future policy and decision-making.

- **Embed learning in funding systems**

Funders and commissioners should prioritise learning as a way to manage the Change Paradox. This means reviewing practice to ensure learning is encouraged and supported, both within funded organisations and within the commissioning body.

This must be done consistently, with consistent messages. Sometimes funders' practices undermine their stated intent. For example, funders might require funded organisations to report on their activity and outcomes in the belief that this encourages learning to be identified and shared. But if organisations perceive reporting primarily as a means for funders to hold them to account, they are unlikely to be open about the challenges they faced or share their learning.

So, make it clear that you are interested in learning about what doesn't work. Provide flexible terms and conditions to encourage innovation and avoid holding people to account for targets and activities. What matters is whether an impact was made and whether learning was generated. Time passes and things change from the time an application is submitted to the time work gets underway. It is better to encourage projects to share these changes with you than to hold them to account for not doing exactly what they set out to.

Again, it is worth checking the language you use to ensure it is consistent with your intent – if you 'monitor' funding and check 'compliance' you are unlikely to get much learning and innovation in return.

- **Encourage honesty**

Even without the requirement to report to external partners, some managers and management practices discourage honesty about unsuccessful interventions. Organisations that characterise such opportunities for learning as 'failure' are, ironically but thankfully, doomed to fail. So, funders should make it clear in their funding systems that they prioritise learning. Application templates and guidance should enquire not just about work that will be undertaken but the learning that will take place. They should not just ask about how a project and its outcomes will be evaluated, but the overarching evaluation or research questions that will be explored. Review meetings and report templates should also encourage reflexivity and honesty about what works and what doesn't.

- **Encourage experimentation and risk-taking**

Policy makers and funders also need to assess their appetite for risk, keeping in mind that in an unsustainable system the risks involved in staying the same are *greater than* the risks of changing. Enlisting the support of partners in policy implementation and commissioning provides you with live, affordable research and development opportunities that, apart from anything else, will enhance your own sustainability. So, encourage experimentation and involve partners in evaluating the results. Be open to novel approaches. Seek out creative partners who can help push your organisation or policies beyond their comfort zone.

- **Create impact and learning reports**

Funders should practice what they preach and produce their own reports about impact and learning. This supports a sustainable sector by sharing intelligence about the effectiveness of different interventions, which can inform other funders' practice and influence policy. It will also inform future applications – and the future funding decisions you make. It also models good practice, showing the transparency that every organisation should have in its approach to reporting.

With non-profit organisations being at the forefront of identifying emerging situations and developing new responses to them, there is not always an evidence base for the different interventions that might be made. But a significant evidence base does exist within commissioning and funding bodies, as they have an overview of the sector from the applications and reports they receive and from their everyday interactions with the organisations they support. It is important not to let this valuable intelligence evaporate. By creating impact reports of their own, funders play a valuable role in distilling learning and sustaining a changing sector.

- **Resist over-specification**

For the reasons above, it will become less common for funders to prescribe activities and outcomes for a fund or the projects they support. If the aim of an intervention is learning, it makes sense to leave space for learning to emerge.

Funders and commissioners should not over-specify the requirements of their programmes. For example, they should be particularly cautious about mandating particular sorts of intervention and activity, as this assumes they know more about local needs than funded organisations do. They might think they are mitigating risk by detailing requirements and monitoring compliance with them. But this actually creates other risks. It limits responsiveness to complex or emerging needs, inhibits creativity and learning, and most importantly, creates mutual distrust that can be very hard to undo.

Instead, focus on what you want to learn and achieve. Build trusting relationships with partners who share your aims and be open to the ideas and energy they will be delighted to bring when you give them the space to do so. This approach helps address the Change Paradox because it is more suitable for adaptation within complex environments than traditional top-down approaches where outcomes and activities are pre-determined and prescribed. As noted, it requires funders to be confident enough to allow that they don't have all the answers, and to be comfortable about enlisting support. It also means acknowledging the power imbalances otherwise inherent in the funding relationship and addressing them.

Prioritising learning helps to achieve this by reminding all parties that the funding relationship is not simply transactional, but one of mutual exchange between equal partners, each with something to offer.

The risks involved in staying the same are greater than the risks of changing.

Board responses to the Change Paradox

- **Accept that uncertainty and risk are different things**

Change is often associated with uncertainty and risk. But when we accept that change is certain, and that the systems in which we operate are becoming unsustainable, a new truth emerges. The risks of not changing outweigh the risks of change. Boards that remember this and identify their level of tolerance for risk will help their organisations to manage the Change Paradox. They will plan for appropriate development, make room for discovery, and manage risk rather than seeking to eliminate it.

- **Ensure stability and adaptability are in balance**

Boards must act as guardians of their organisation's core purpose, remembering that its aims may never change, but that almost everything else will. This means accepting that although stability and predictability might seem desirable, they are unlikely to occur, and if they do, it won't be for long. And that's no bad thing. If an organisation seems stable and predictable it's probably stagnating. As the people responsible for the organisation's *direction*, trustees must help to develop the organisation's openness to change. Boards should discuss how to find the balance between providing a stable and predictable working environment and encouraging learning, adaptability and change.

Part of this will depend on a board's ability to develop a culture of trust, where change is pursued purposefully, and appropriate levels of experimentation and risk are encouraged. This includes having clear strategic plans but accepting that they will never be realised exactly as intended. Some plans won't come off. Unanticipated opportunities will emerge. Sustainable organisations learn from and respond to these events, balancing strategic intent with pragmatic opportunism. Of course, this means having ways of identifying which opportunities to pursue and which to abandon, something we will say more about when addressing the Octopus Paradox.

Management responses to the Change Paradox

- **Experiment, fail and learn**

When new initiatives succeed, managers should identify opportunities for the project to be scaled up and spread if appropriate – not all sustainability challenges are about survival, some are about growth. When initiatives fail, managers should make sure the impact on beneficiaries, staff and other stakeholders (including the organisation itself) is minimised. In each case, identifying, responding to and sharing learning is crucial to managing the paradox of change because it is only by learning that organisations can keep up with the pace of change. When things are going well, managers can learn about emerging needs and opportunities, anticipating trends and positioning their organisation to make the most of them. When things aren't going well or when experiments fail, managers who see this as a learning opportunity ensure mistakes are not repeated and that losses aren't final or fatal.

- **Embed learning**

Managers should help their organisations remain responsive and adaptable by ensuring that learning is integrated into every level and system within the organisation. They should think of projects as experiments, pilots, or small tests of change, with exit strategies and communication plans in place at an early stage. This will help them to manage the continuation or closure of projects as appropriate.

- **Plan for exit**

For organisations or interventions where the intention is to build capacity in individuals, communities or organisations, managers will need to plan for exit from the outset. Has the intervention been based on an issue identified by the people it belongs to? What would effective capacity look like once it has been built? Who will the work belong to once it is done? [See Part 5 for more on exit strategies].

Operational responses to the Change Paradox

- **Sensing change and sharing intelligence**

Operational teams have a key role in sensing and responding to change. Being the organisation's main interface with the external environment, staff have a unique, privileged perspective on how well the organisation's plans and strategies match up to stakeholder requirements. Learning should be a core part of their work alongside delivery:

- Listening to stakeholders
- Identifying and developing responses to unmet need/demand
- Reflecting on their practice
- Evaluating the impact of their work
- Sharing ideas and learning with colleagues and managers.

Sadly, this is often far from being the case. Boards and senior managers may use the old cliché about '*staff being our most important resource*' but this is really a euphemism for '*staff are our biggest expense*'. If staff were the most important resource then the organisation's core work wouldn't be done by lowest paid, least qualified people. Managers wouldn't talk about cascading information 'down' to staff, or boards and management being at 'the top'. Organisational charts wouldn't be drawn with boards on top like the angels on a Christmas tree. Instead, the organisation would be understood in terms of the flow of learning and intelligence, with staff at the nodes, learning from the environment and passing data to the centre where it can be analysed and shared – see Figure 4.

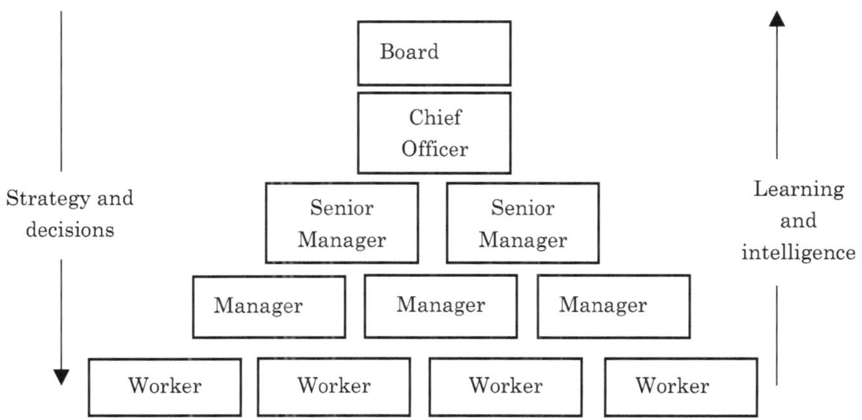

Figure 4: The traditional organisational chart could be turned upside down to show frontline workers' roles in generating and funneling learning.

Charles Handy famously characterised four types of organisational structure and culture, identifying that hierarchical bureaucracies like those in Figure 4 are useful for managing stability. Many organisations have sought to develop similar structures as part of their growth away from being small projects (sometimes led by a charismatic or dominant founder). Formalising systems and developing processes help to manage growth and mitigate risk. Staff have clearly defined roles and operate within clear parameters. I use the metaphor of a chess board for this: The King and Queen rule the board. Like each chess piece, staff roles have certain attributes and they only move in pre-defined ways. But as Handy rightly identified, these structures are not good at coping with change or complexity, the very challenges we now face.

- **Reflection and learning**

To cope effectively with the Change Paradox and contribute to sustainability, operational staff need to work within supportive organisational learning environments. They must have time and opportunities to reflect on and develop their practice. I liken this to a draughts board, where each piece can go in any direction in response to moves that develop as the game gets played.

This requires staff to be supported to develop and learn:

- How to identify stakeholder needs and develop responses
- How to plan, review and evaluate activities
- When and how to share the learning that emerges.

In this way of working, organisations use one-to-one and team meetings, training and appraisal not as opportunities to tell staff what to do, but to identify and distil learning that can be shared across the organisation.

These ideas are not controversial and managers intuitively understand the value of them. But times are tough. At the time of writing, western countries have had ten years of government austerity programmes, with cuts to non-profit funding, services and staffing only set to increase over at least the medium term. When organisations are under severe pressure just to survive it sounds ridiculous to talk about having time to think, and about learning being as important as delivery.

But the fact that organisations are caught in a bind, despite knowing the challenges and some of the answers, only highlights the urgency of creating the capacity to respond to change. We continue to explore this in the remaining paradoxes.

Reminder

The Change Paradox: Only by changing can organisations be sustainable.

Principle: Sustainability does not mean 'sustained'.

Practice: Learn, adapt and evolve purposefully.

System-level responses to the Change Paradox

- Prioritise and encourage system learning
- Embed learning in funding systems
- Encourage honesty
- Encourage experimentation and risk-taking
- Create impact and learning reports
- Resist over-specification

Board responses to the Change Paradox

- Accept that uncertainty and risk are different things
- Ensure stability and adaptability are in balance

Management responses to the Change Paradox

- Experiment, fail and learn
- Embed organisational learning
- Plan for exit

Operational responses to the Change Paradox

- Sense change and share intelligence
- Reflect and learn

CHAPTER 5: THE OCTOPUS PARADOX

The Octopus Paradox: Organisations need to reach out in new directions to grow. But growing in too many directions pulls them out of shape.

This paradox arises because of the Change Paradox. When organisations need to change to survive, they reach out in new directions, growing new projects like tentacles, in search of new opportunities.

Most organisations would like to reduce risk and increase sustainability by diversifying their sources of income. But because non-profit funding is typically focused on activity, and many funders only support new or 'innovative' activity, organisations wanting to diversify their income need to diversify their activities. Although it frustrates non-profits, this approach is also rooted in the Change Paradox. Funders want to support organisations that can evidence that they are learning, changing and evolving.

Diversifying activity can result in organisations becoming octopus-shaped, reaching out a tentacle towards this funding pot over here, reaching out another to that field of work over there. For example, when I managed a volunteering programme, the city in which I worked developed a programme to invest millions of pounds in employability projects. It was very tempting to reach out a tentacle (i.e. a project) in that direction – we could evidence the links between our volunteering programme and people's employability. But volunteering is also about people wanting to give something back to communities, to be among other people, or to maintain a level of health and fitness. If we grew a tentacle in each of these directions, seeking support from funders in the employability, community development and health sectors, we might grow for a time. But we would also risk spreading ourselves too thinly and diluting our core purpose. Long term we would probably regret stretching so far.

Over time as organisations grow organically in response to opportunities that come their way, organisational tentacles grow further apart from the body - and away from each other. This leads to projects or services feeling separate from or forgotten by the organisation that hosts them, or organisations feeling they've lost 'control'. These aren't necessarily bad things. As noted within the operational responses to the Change Paradox, dispersed teams can generate a lot of learning and intelligence to help organisations adapt and respond to the complex world around them. But instead, teams often end up opposing or competing with each other (or the host organisation) because they are looking and moving in different directions. In the volunteering example above, a team focused on employability would have quite different goals and priorities to a team supporting community development.

One of the problems is that as the tentacles grow, the head and body get smaller. They might get smaller purely in proportion to the tentacles, or they might actually shrink because there is less funding available for core overhead costs like administration, management, personnel support etc. One way or another, many organisations report having less capacity at the centre to manage and administer their increasingly diverse projects. There comes a time when this becomes unsustainable. That's when organisations need to step back and review their core purpose, to pull in their tentacles. This is the most common strategy non-profits have taken in the years since the financial crisis in 2008. Sustainable organisations know what they do best, and they know what to let go of.

Overview – the Paradox in brief

The Octopus paradox: Organisations need to reach out in new directions to grow. But growing in too many directions pulls them out of shape.

Principle: Diversified income does not mean reduced risk.

Practice: Focus on core organisational purpose and structure.

System-level responses to the Octopus Paradox

- **Acknowledge the ways that systems encourage octopuses to grow**

Commissioners and policy makers need to acknowledge their role in creating octopus-shaped organisations.

At a policy level, new policies and strategies can pull non-profit organisations out of shape, sometimes even requiring contradictory actions from them. It resembles the magic trick where the nimble assistant is placed in a sealed box which the magician then thrusts swords into from different angles. Non-profit organisations have to become extraordinarily agile in adjusting to the policy and legislative 'swords' that come at them from different directions

> *For example, in recent years implementing the UK Living Wage required many social care organisations to increase staff salaries, while European procurement directives required commissioners to get the best value for money. Commissioners' reluctance or inability to increase contract funding has led to organisations unsustainably subsidising contracts – or withdrawing from them. This in turn leads to a less diverse market, putting pressure on the same commissioners, who have a statutory responsibility to ensure there is a sufficient supply of different services. While all this was going on, new care legislation was enacted, care standards were published, condition-specific strategies were launched and updated, guidance on protecting adults and children was produced – and so on.*

While policy measures are important individually, when they are implemented individually, without anticipating their collective or systemic effect, they have a negative impact on sector sustainability. Policy-makers should work with non-profit organisations to check the sector's capacity and readiness for new developments. Participatory policy-making, involving organisations throughout the stages of design and implementation, will help to ensure the sector is not pulled out of shape in unsustainable ways.

- **Stop the funding merry-go-round**

The Octopus Paradox mostly stems from the practice of privileging new initiatives rather than providing repeat or continuation funding. There are good reasons why so many funders take this approach. It ensures their monies reach as many organisations as possible over time. It helps ensure that services are based on recently-identified need. And it encourages the piloting and testing of new approaches, something which is very valuable for sustainability, as we will see when exploring the Efficiency Paradox.

However, it is also done in the belief that funders' money is best spent pump-priming new initiatives, like investment capital is used in the for-profit sector. This is an exciting way to fund, allowing funders to help interesting new ideas get off the ground. This is very alluring, particularly for chief executives, who are often on the look out for new ideas and opportunities. But it is a belief founded on a fallacy. The fallacy is that if the project is good enough, another funder will step in to sustain it once the start-up funding ends. But of course, funders are interested in new initiatives, not continuation funding...

The legacy of this is a condition known as 'projectitis', the swelling and proliferation of quasi-projects designed more to fit into funding criteria than to test or learn anything. Often they are existing projects disguised as new ones purely to meet funders' criteria.

Funders know that these practices go on, and sadly they sometimes think that's what sustainability is – the ability of an organisation to get funding from Funder B when Funder A's money runs out. This is not a systemic approach to sustainability. It's actually one of the primary *causes* of sustainability challenges in the sector, requiring non-profit organisations to expend huge amounts of time and effort keeping up with the merry-go-round.

- **Explore what sustainable funding means in a particular context**

Funders cannot and should not fund the same organisations indefinitely. The Change Paradox tells us that. But systemic responses to the Octopus Paradox are possible. Fundamentally, it requires anyone who distributes funding to explore what sustainable funding looks like, which can include:

- Policy makers being alert to the scale and pace of change in their sector and responding accordingly.
- Funders aligning their work to prevailing developments in the policy environment, so their work faces in a similar direction.
- Policy-makers seeking out emerging evidence from funders and developing policy responses to funders' impact reports.
- Funding a balanced portfolio, for example of short-life projects and longer-term interventions to address deep-rooted challenges.
- Funding continuing work where evidence exists of learning and development.
- Requiring applicants to align their core outcomes to the fund, rather than adding the fund's outcomes to their own.
- Rejecting funding applications which show signs of projects being funding-led (e.g. poor strategic fit, questionable capacity to deliver, large organisations applying for small projects with no clear learning intent).
- Facilitating networks of funded organisations, for sharing practice, generating learning or encouraging collaboration.

- **Develop funding and market shaping strategies**

Some of the measures in the list above could be considered as part of a 'market shaping' strategy. Market shaping (also known as market facilitation) is a system-level approach which seeks to contribute to the sustainability – or avoid the collapse - of a particular market or field of work. To do this, policy makers, funders and commissioners work with local communities and non-profit organisations to:

- Understand current, unmet or emerging needs, mapping existing provision and identifying gaps.
- Devise strategies and co-design interventions to meet these needs.
- Deliver the interventions.
- Review and evaluate interventions against the original strategic goals and any new evidence or emerging trends.

Publishing the resulting strategies (whether funding strategies or market shaping strategies) allows potential partners and grant applicants to understand the strategic intent behind an intervention and make informed decisions about whether to align with that intent. This helps to avoid pulling non-profit organisations out of shape – or growing tentacles in unsustainable directions.

Crucially, the market shaping process allows withdrawals from previous commissioning strategies and commitments to be planned and communicated in advance. This gives stakeholders time to adjust and helps prevent the sudden collapse of local economies or organisations. It also forestalls community anxiety or antipathy, helping people to understand (or be involved in decisions about) why certain provision is or isn't being commissioned.

Board responses to the Octopus Paradox

- **Provide strong leadership**

Boards need strong leadership to avoid the mission drift that comes with the Octopus Paradox. And in my experience, they are usually good at using the organisation's core purposes as touchstones in decision-making. At the same time, trustees want to be helpful, and one of the most common ways to try to be helpful is to make suggestions, typically for new areas of activity or development. Despite trustees' best intentions, this can be unhelpful for lots of reasons:

- It assumes they have enough operating knowledge of the organisation to know what sorts of activity are more effective than others
- It assumes managers haven't already identified or explored ideas, risking patronising and alienating them.
- It crosses the line between governance and management.

- **Develop an income generation strategy**

Another important way for boards to show leadership of the Octopus Paradox is to ensure the organisation has an income generation strategy in place. This should identify the organisation's current and desired funding mix, and the strategies and messages for engaging with different 'markets' (e.g. the main sources of revenue like donations, grants, contracts, trading and corporate sponsorship). An effective income generation strategy needs to align closely with the strategic plan and encompass any marketing, communications, fundraising and business development strategies that exist. (The reasons for this are explained in Chapter 12 on Income Generation).

Too often, organisations react to funding opportunities without having clear criteria for making decisions about them, other than to believe that any money is good money.

I once made a presentation to a conference of professional fundraisers. One of them raised their hand when I talked about the Octopus Paradox and asked how they could get their manager to understand this. The week before, the manager had come to the fundraiser and said, *'I need you to raise £1m this year.'* The fundraiser knew that to persuade donors and funders to part with their money, she would need to be able to describe what the money was for and what difference it would make. So, quite rightly, she asked the manager what the £1m was for. *'What's it for?'* the manager repeated incredulously, *'It's for £1m, that's what it's for!'*. What an octopus!

Seeking money without clear strategies for what it will – and will not – be used for is a guarantee of mission drift. For an organisation that believes all money is good money, it will do anything as long as it attracts revenue. This is a mistake for two reasons. Firstly, it will almost inevitably pull the organisation off course and dilute its identity and purpose. Secondly, it commits the organisation to the pursuit of unsustainable growth. Take the example above and let's imagine the fundraiser was successful at raising the desired £1m. It will need to be raised again the following year, and the year after. Sustainability will become nothing more than the pursuit of survival, putting growth above people and purpose. Which is not why non-profit organisations exist. Sooner or later, the dissonance between the organisation's stated purpose and actual practice will lead to sustainability challenges arising from lack of focus, confused identity, disillusioned staff and stakeholders and competition for market share.

- **Be aware of investment and risk**

Some sources and types of revenue are worth more than others. As pressure on grant-makers' and commissioners' budgets grows, organisations are increasingly being expected to contribute to the costs of projects and interventions. Boards should think very carefully about accepting funding on this basis. Yes, they represent non-profit organisations, whose job it is to use their funds to make a difference. But boards should always have clear strategic reasons for subsidising the costs of any venture. They may choose to subsidise activities that support the organisation's mission. Or they may subsidise costs to help the organisation become established in a new market or to undercut competitors. However, there is only one way that a strategy of charging below costs can end: bankruptcy.

This isn't to say that boards should have a blanket ban on approving deficit budgets (if they did, many non-profits would go out of business overnight due to the financial uncertainty in which they operate) or subsidising the public purse. But they should always be aware that this is what they are doing. They should treat it as an investment and identify risks, expected returns and how they will be measured and managed. This is explored further in Chapter 12 on Income Generation.

Trustees can also help to manage the Octopus Paradox by answering these questions:

'How much of one thing are we prepared to forego in order to achieve something else?'
Sustainable strategy means acknowledging that, when it comes to finite resources like time, effort and money, more of something means less of something else. This can be hard for trustees to accept. Understandably, they want their organisations to develop. But trustees' roles require them to make tough decisions about how resources can best be used to achieve organisational goals. When it is proposed to grow a tentacle in a new direction, trustees should be sure that there is a need for it and that it can be resourced. They should also discuss how the growth will be managed and measured. Will staff time be created or freed for development work? If so, will other duties have to be foregone? How will the 'tentacle' be managed? Does the body of the organisation have the spare capacity to support it, or are more resources needed? Chief officers are unlikely to want to admit that they cannot deliver what boards ask for, so trustees must support them to review and manage their capacity realistically.

'How much is enough?'
Boards are used to receiving comprehensive reports about activity, budgets, achievement of objectives and so on. But they are less used to having the information contextualised – what do the figures mean? Are they high or low, good or bad? This is partly a simple reminder that trustees need information on trends, so information should be presented in ways that help this (for example, with last year's figures shown alongside this year's). But it's mostly a reminder for boards to be clear on what success looks like.

I've witnessed countless boards listen to presentations and read reports only to follow up with the question 'Is this enough?'. Let's take the example of a charity supporting children with autism. Maybe it has helped hundreds of children in one part of the country, but the board might ask how many it planned to reach. How many more children with autism are there locally? And what about further afield, wouldn't it be nice to reach children in different parts of the country?

A key way boards can avoid the octopus is to be very clear on how much is 'enough'. Define goals clearly at the outset, understand the limits of the resources available (including staffing) and accept that there will always be unmet need, there will always be more to do.

Management responses to the Octopus Paradox

- **Provide clarity and alignment**

To avoid the octopus, managers should make sure that staff and board perceptions of the organisation's mission, aims and values are aligned. Is the organisation's strategy clear and easy to follow? Does it mean the same thing to people throughout the organisation? A manager's role here is to embed strategic aims in such a way that they are brought to life in people's work.

Keeping strategic plans short and visual helps trustees, staff, volunteers and clients really buy into them. There's a lot to be said for being able to express purpose and strategy succinctly). Some organisations have shared their examples on the Lasting Difference website. You can view these and do the same by visiting www.TheLastingDifference.com.

- **Engage with the policy and funding environment**

As noted above, managers should develop income generation strategies where financial goals can be contained (in both senses of the word). These strategies should be holistic, to include chief officers' roles in influencing long-term income generation opportunities. The work they do in lobbying, influencing policy and contributing to local or national government strategies helps to create the environment in which services will operate and be funded in the medium to long-term. If successful, this also helps to tame the octopus, aligning the internal and external policy environments. This kind of external influencing should be included in the income generation strategy, so its purposes are recognised and remembered not just by chief officers, but by boards. Trustees are often curious about the amount of time chief officers spend outside the organisation. Some trustees believe chief officers should be like the hood ornament on a fancy car – outside, up front, looking forward. Others are wary, sometimes even suspicious of this, needing reassurance that managers are at the wheel with a careful eye on the road, the map and the instrument panel (particularly the fuel gauge and speedometer)! Whatever approach is taken to senior level engagement with the policy and funding environment, it makes sense to have a clear sustainability rationale behind it.

- **Develop idea screening matrices and protocols**

One of the most useful ways of taming the octopus is to use a matrix for screening ideas. This can help to identify when current or potential working methods, projects and funding opportunities weaken sustainability. It can also help relieve pressure on staff, who often internalise a great deal of pressure to take on more and more work.

Developing and using such a matrix can help staff and managers to critically review and select from the range of activities and opportunities available.

Some organisations have generously shared examples of what goes into their decision-making matrices on the Lasting Difference website. Any organisation can custom build their own, ideally with trustees, managers and staff working together to identify the criteria to use for making decisions. As well as checking alignment with organisation strategy and values, the matrix should also assess the impact of new or potential ideas on:

- Clients and communities.
- The capacity of staff – and staffing levels.
- Skills and knowledge (these are often overlooked when boards consider the resources the organisation needs to implement a new strategy. Although trustee skills audits are quite commonplace, examples of organisational knowledge audits are surprisingly rare in knowledge-age workplaces).
- Management – capacity to develop and/or oversee the work.
- Quality and effectiveness – what difference will the idea make? What outcomes will be achieved?
- Resources – what approach will the organisation take to projects that don't cover full costs, or require investment?
- Relationships and reputation e.g. with funders/commissioners/partners.
- Organisational learning – does the opportunity dilute organisational strengths or enhance them? Does it add to or diminish specialisms? Does it increase or decrease value?

- **Privilege learning**

The last bullet in the list above is a sustainability deal-breaker. Of course, organisations should select those opportunities that serve their core purposes and communities best. But beyond that, if they are not sure which tentacles to grow and which to retract, the Change Paradox tells us that the ability to learn should be retained and developed above all else. Sustainability decisions aren't just about selecting *what* to sustain, but about the sustaining the *ability* to test, learn and change.

So, organisations should prioritise projects, activities and opportunities that help them to *learn*.

This might seem obvious, but imagine I gave you 10% of your organisation's revenue to do whatever you like with. What would you do with it? Sustainable organisations use unrestricted funds like this to invest in testing and learning from new approaches and initiatives.

If I gave you 10% of your organisation's revenue to do whatever you like with, what would you do with it? Sustainable organisations use unrestricted funds like this to invest in new initiatives.

Operational responses to the Octopus Paradox

Despite what we have said about the disadvantages of having too many, or too large, tentacles, it's useful to think about how an octopus swims. It propels itself forward with its tentacles, not its head. Projects are how organisations can respond to emerging need, testing new approaches and generating learning to propel themselves forward. Operational staff can therefore help to tame the Octopus Paradox in several ways.

- **Align and screen ideas**

Firstly, they need to understand the organisational and income generation strategies described above. They should use (or develop) an idea screening matrix, to help identify and say no to opportunities that detract from organisational purpose, capacity or sustainability. Staff can build sustainability in from the start of the project by running their plans through the matrix before submitting funding applications.

It is worth noting that most UK grant funders' application processes ask about how the work will be sustained once funding ends. What better way to address the question than to say that a sustainability assessment has already been carried out? [It is also interesting to note that although I have presented to and trained dozens of funding bodies on sustainability, only a few have been able to explain why they ask the sustainability question. They don't ask it to get an answer – they know the question is almost unanswerable. But they want to signal to applicants that the money will indeed end, and that preparations should be made for this from the outset.]

- **Reflect on practice**

As with the Change Paradox, the Octopus Paradox can be mitigated by staff actively evaluating and reporting on their work as part of their everyday practice (not just at the end of a piece of work).

This helps to fulfil the organisation's original learning intention behind developing the project. But, particularly within large organisations, it's also about making sure colleagues, management and trustees know that the project, service or business unit exists – and matters. To be sustainable, projects and services sometimes have an internal marketing job to do before even starting to look outside the organisation. This isn't about competing with or shouting louder than other services but making sure the organisation can make informed decisions based on understanding the value of each of its operations. For large and international non-profit organisations, it's probably more accurate to talk about jellyfish tendrils, which can number in the hundreds, than octopus tentacles.

- **Share learning**

It is important that staff take or create opportunities to share what they learn in their projects and services with colleagues across and outside the organisation. This definitely includes writing the reports that funders, managers and trustees expect. But to generate buy-in for sustainability it's ideal to get people face to face. Staff should therefore attend, and ideally host, cross-team meetings, multi-agency events and site visits to showcase and share learning. They should host or participate in communities of practice, learning exchanges, workshops and become known as experts in their field by running training, giving conference inputs, writing, blogging or sharing ideas via social media. As with the idea of the chief officer as hood ornament, this all contributes to shaping the environment and therefore taming the octopus.

- **Work together towards sustainability**

Depending on the culture and approach taken within each organisation, staff might also want to convene or take part in a sustainability working group; develop sustainability plans for their teams; or use quarterly or annual appraisal to report on their contributions to organisational strategy and sustainability.

Reminder

The Octopus paradox: Organisations need to reach out in new directions to grow. But growing in too many directions pulls them out of shape.

Principle: Diversified income does not mean reduced risk.

Practice: Focus on core organisational purpose and structure.

System-level responses to the Octopus Paradox

- Acknowledge the ways that systems encourage octopuses to grow
- Stop the funding merry-go-round
- Explore what sustainable funding means in a particular context
- Develop funding and market shaping strategies

Board responses to the Octopus Paradox

- Provide strong leadership
- Develop income generation strategies
- Be aware of investment and risk

Management responses to the Octopus Paradox

- Provide clarity and alignment
- Engage with the policy and funding environment
- Develop idea screening matrices and protocols
- Privilege learning

Operational responses to the Octopus Paradox

- Align and screen ideas
- Reflect on practice
- Share learning
- Work together towards sustainability

CHAPTER 6: THE YES/NO PARADOX

The Yes/No Paradox: The things that an organisation needs to survive can also kill it. Saying 'yes' to everything is fatal.

This paradox manifests in organisations when they can't say no to the things that should help them to survive, but which can have toxic effects on their sustainability. Things like referrals, funding, development opportunities, partnership requests etc.

When organisations think they will be more sustainable by saying 'yes' to everything, they are actually doing the opposite. They are diminishing their sustainability and chances of survival. Paradoxically, those who say 'no' usually confidently describe how it improved their organisation's health.

Think of organisations like a balloon. Uninflated, the skin isn't stretched, with lots of capacity to expand. But this capacity is finite. Each time the organisation says 'yes' the balloon inflates and grows. Its skin stretches to accommodate the new air. The pressure increases. There is only so much air that can be put in a balloon before the skin gets stretched too tight. Unless the pressure is released, sooner or later the balloon will burst.

The Yes/No Paradox is about managing capacity.

We might not think it is possible to work beyond our capacity. We might laugh (or groan) when we hear interviews with sports stars describing how they are going to 'give 110%' to the team. However, if safety, quality and staff wellbeing matter (and of course they matter immensely), many of our colleagues and organisations are indeed working beyond their capacity. Common examples include:

- Developing new pieces of work while previous developments are left to flounder.
- Taking on work without having enough staff capacity to deliver.
- Agreeing funding or contracts that don't cover their full costs.
- Using waiting lists in order to 'accept' referrals the service doesn't have time to consider, or space to accommodate.
- Staff working beyond contracted hours and allowing or expecting colleagues to do the same.

In fact, the most common sustainability challenge comes from saying 'yes' too often. Another way of expressing the paradox is that many organisations are less sustainable *because* of saying yes, not in spite of it.

The most common sustainability challenge comes from saying 'yes' too often. Many organisations are less sustainable because of saying yes, not in spite of it.

If this makes you feel uncomfortable, ask yourself *'Do I regret saying yes more than I regret saying no?'*. When I use this question in workshops and conference presentations the sound of pennies dropping is almost audible. In a way, it's a trick question – I know that people won't have a lot of practice of saying no in their careers. The non-profit world thrives on having highly committed people like this. But we must also accept that in many organisations staff could work 24 hours a day and it still would not be enough to deal with all of the issues they are trying to address. Much as we might like to think we're superheroes, there comes a point, individually and collectively, where we can't give any more. A sad aspect of this paradox is that while non-profit organisations are all about caring about issues and people, they're not always good at applying that care to their own staff.

There may be many reasons why we say 'yes'. As people and organisations driven by purpose, we want to help. It's not nice to disappoint people or feel guilty for not helping. And if we're honest, it feels good to be needed. There might also be darker motivations – what if someone else says yes and we miss out? This competitiveness drives many of our decisions. But at its root, the main reason organisations say yes is that they believe they will be less sustainable if they say no.

Examples of this belief in action are listed below, along with illustrations from experience of why they are probably mistaken.

Belief	Experience
External: Funders will not support us in future if we turn down their money now.	Funders want to fund effective work. They want to reduce the burdens on non-profit organisations, not add to them. They respect good governance and decision-making.
External: Referrers will stop referring to us if we close our doors.	Referrers are busy too, experiencing the same pressures you do. Knowing you are prioritising the people or issues they have already entrusted you with, before taking more on, will reassure them.
Organisational: Our reputation will be affected if we say no.	Your organisation's reputation will be affected if it says yes and doesn't deliver. What does it want to be known for? For quality and integrity or for being prepared to accept anything?
Organisational: We might regret saying no.	You might, but you don't know for sure. But you know for sure that you'll regret saying yes to everything.
Individual: People will think I'm a bad person, incompetent or unable to cope.	People value honesty and it's dishonest not to say when you don't have the capacity to take something on.

Table 1: Beliefs and experience of saying 'no'.

It's extremely hard to say no and we need lots of reassurance and practice before feeling confident that it's the right thing to do. For this reason, during workshops and conferences I often ask if anyone is willing to share an example of saying 'No' and what happened. On *every* occasion, people describe it being the hardest decision they or their organisation had to make – but the right one. They may have temporarily closed their doors to referrals, going against the very reason they exist and risking their reputation with referrers. Maybe the example was of not pursuing a funding bid, which risked upsetting the funder – or trustees with a keen eye on the balance sheet. Maybe they turned down an invitation to form a new partnership, putting relationships with stakeholders at risk. Or maybe the organisation needed to restructure, making decisions about which services to close and which posts to make redundant. But the speakers always end the story by saying that time has shown them that these were the right decisions to take. In every case they and their organisations have not only lived to tell the tale, they were stronger for it. The world didn't end.

It's not enough for organisations to monitor the pressure in the balloon. They already know when they are working beyond capacity, from metrics like staff absence, retention and turnover rates; referral rates; client waiting times; project lead-in times and completion rates; accident and incident reports; user satisfaction and so on. Instead, they need to release the pressure. People at all levels must be confident and supported to say 'no'.

Overview – The Paradox in brief

The Yes/No Paradox: The things that an organisation needs to survive can also kill it. Saying 'yes' to everything is fatal.

Principle: Sustainability is about more than just money. Capacity and quality matter.

Practices: Understand when, how and what to say 'no' to.

System-level responses to the Yes/No Paradox

- **Assess system and sector sustainability**

Commissioners and policy makers need to monitor the health of the system which they help to create – and which they rely on for results. Non-profit diversity, quality and capacity are important indicators of organisational health.

At a system level, it should be easy to discern whether the number of non-profit organisations in an area is stable, growing, or in decline. Changes and trends need to be interpreted to assess the health of the sector and the trajectory it is on. For example, if there is a decline in the number of organisations in a field, is this a good thing because a need no longer exists, or a bad thing because organisations were unable to attract (or afford) ongoing support, staffing or funding? Other indicators include the quality and number of applications funders receive and the number and nature of organisations that make them.

It is particularly important to look out for any thematic or geographical areas that are under-represented in a funding or policy portfolio and to take action accordingly. Diversity is important to ensure initiatives reach and learn from the full range of people who might be affected. At a system level, diversity in the portfolio also helps ensure sustainability because it reduces reliance on any one model or approach which might prove ineffective as the environment changes.

- **Develop pre-contract relationships and support**

The decision as to whether to commit resources to supporting non-profit organisations *before* the award of a grant or contract is not straightforward. Each funder or commissioner will have their own strategy based on preference and resources. For many, it makes sense to focus limited resources by prioritising post-award relationships and support.

However, pre-application information and support can turn the binary 'Yes/No' paradox into a more productive 'Maybe'. Consultations, exchanges and information events with potential suppliers can build productive relationships based on trust and shared understanding, leading to better longer-term outcomes. Funders and policy makers might even need to make special efforts to engage organisations that don't come forward, as there may be a capacity-building need in a particular community or sector. There may also be institutional barriers, for instance small organisations might not have the time and resources to commit to large funding applications that require research and form filling. They might not be able to tender for large contracts because they lack the capacity to deliver or manage them alone. Providing pre-contract support, coupled with different types and levels of engagement (and funding) can help to overcome this, enabling potentially marginalised organisations to develop their capacity without compromising their core values or purposes.

- **Assess financial viability and reward financial stewardship**

Funders typically assess the financial viability of individual organisations to ensure their money (and reputations) are in safe hands. To support sustainability, they must also assess whether the funding will improve or diminish financial viability.

Organisations are occasionally surprised when funders advise them to apply for more money than they originally requested. They might think the funder is being generous, not realising that funders have good insight about how much activities – and quality – actually cost, and that they don't want to invest in something that will fail due to lack of appropriate resources.

On the other hand, some funders accept sub-optimal delivery when they are not able to award as much money as has been applied for. This might mean accepting smaller scale delivery (e.g. working in fewer places, with fewer people, on a smaller range of issues, or over a shorter time frame). Others will fund direct project costs, but not 'on costs' like pensions, management costs, staff training, evaluation and so on; as if these were somehow frivolous luxuries.

Similarly, if a project costs less than anticipated, many funders will require the unspent monies to be repaid. This is understandable in that it allows funds to go to other worthwhile projects and it helps prevent organisations fraudulently applying for more money than they need. However, it does not reward organisations which have managed their resources effectively, perhaps using their own infrastructure (like management costs, staff training, evaluation systems...) and economies of scale.

In their desperation to manage deficits, some commissioners have even begun to require charities hand over any surplus they make. This assumes that the surplus came from that commissioner's funds alone, not from the other funders or donors a charity will have (who, if they made the same claims, would bankrupt the charity). It penalises sustainable practices like organisational efficiency, prudent management, shrewd investment policies, and the strategic use or sale of assets.

Different funding practices can be imagined along a continuum, from those which require work to be subsidised to those which support the full costs of a project, see Figure 5 below.

Require subsidy to cover direct costs (e.g. from organisation's reserves)	Support direct service costs only	Accept sub-optimal delivery	Require subsidy to cover full costs (e.g. using match funding)	Support full cost recovery	Support full cost recovery, including accrual of reserves

Funding sustainably

Figure 5: Sustaining funding - or funding sustainably?

Any point on the spectrum could be said to sustain funding, i.e. making money go further. For instance, a funder might deem that an organisation has such high levels of unrestricted reserves that it can afford to contribute to project costs. This might be a sensible way of managing the Yes/No Paradox, requiring an organisation to focus on its core purpose. But cases of non-profit organisations having fat reserves are rare (though often well publicised). Good practice requires non-profit organisations to have a sensible reserves policy and enough reserves to meet operating costs, planned commitments, unforeseen costs and to manage uncertainty. Funders should be careful not to penalise prudent organisations.

If funders are interested in funding sustainably, they must support full cost recovery. Requiring match funding can support sustainability by building the funded organisation's capacity to reach new funders. However, there is an extra burden involved in finding, applying and reporting to each new funder, so it is questionable whether this is really a model of funding sustainably. (Examples do exist of funders working in partnership to harmonise their processes or integrate their funds, which can reduce some of the burden of duplicate applications and reporting requirements).

Board responses to the Yes/No Paradox

- **Retain clarity of purpose**

Boards need to ensure the organisation has clarity of purpose and strategy. The risk in having missions that are too broad, or poorly defined, is not just that they won't be achieved, but that the organisation will be harmed as it strains to fulfil them.

A trustee's role is to act in the organisation's best interest and safeguard its future. This means attending to capacity, the quality of its work and the wellbeing of its people.

- **Manage capacity**

To help manage capacity, trustees need to manage contradictions between what they say and what they do. There's no point in trustees saying they want managers to work within their capacity and not take too much on, while still expecting more from them. Boards can't just pay lip service to managing capacity like this. Even where boards give clear consistent messages about capacity, managers and staff will almost certainly internalise a pressure to do more and to say yes to everything. Boards must actively support people to say no, not just giving permission but requiring it – and living happily with the consequences. For example, in my company we log all the potential opportunities we say no to or don't go for. For each of the last five years the total value of work we don't take on has been the same as our turnover. In other words, if we took on every opportunity that came along we could double in size. But even though we're a 'for profit' company, there are good reasons why we're not interested in growing in that way. Sustainability is about more than just money. Quality and reputation matter. Capacity matters. Purpose matters.

To manage the Yes/No Paradox, boards must stand back from the detail of services, ideas and opportunities and check the organisation really has the capacity to take them on and manage them effectively.

Management responses to the Yes/No Paradox

- **Monitor and report on capacity**

I once worked in an organisation which was really struggling for capacity. It had been through a hard time, resulting in changes in management and high turnover of staff. The manager had asked a colleague to work more than their allotted hours that week to help get through some outstanding work. The colleague discussed it with me, before concluding that although they wanted to help, they were not prepared to. When I asked why, they simply said 'Because that would mask the problem.' In their view, the more that staff worked beyond their hours, the less likely the board and the organisation's funders would be to know there was a problem and to help address it.

Managing the Yes/No Paradox requires managers to be honest first with themselves then with trustees and funders about workload and capacity. Managers need the honesty to do this and courage to raise capacity challenges. To do this, it helps to be able to evidence the true costs of the work, and the impacts of the capacity issue. This cannot be done if staff and management are used to masking the problem. Nevertheless, it can be hard to raise concerns if they arise directly from changes or conditions attached to the policies, funding or contracts that you work within.

Membership of a trade body or sector intermediary, which can represent the views of organisations, can help issues like these be raised in depersonalised ways.

- **Support staff to work within capacity**

In the same way that board messages must be congruent with the practical support they give, so must managers'. There's no point in a manager encouraging colleagues to leave work on time then emailing them in the evening or weekend. Whatever they say, people will see these behaviours and take them as tacit permission or encouragement to do the same. If managers want to encourage healthy working patterns, they must work healthily. This is one occasion where leading by example actually works.

- **Identify personal values**

Even with board support, managers will probably feel high levels of internally or externally-located pressure to take on more work. Managing this requires being clear on who they are as professionals, but also as people.
A group of managers I worked with at a leadership workshop came up with questions about their 'values', which can have three different meanings in this context:

- ***What do you believe in?***
- ***What do you place value upon?***
- ***What is your own value?***

These and some of the questions in the section below can help to manage the Yes/No Paradox and the capacity challenges that managers encounter daily.

Operational responses to the Yes/No Paradox

- **Knowing what to say 'yes' to**

Staff at all levels need to know what they can safely to say yes to. The short strategic plan and the idea screening matrix mentioned in the Octopus Paradox can help with this. Do they know the parameters within which they can make decisions about the work and opportunities they take on?

Operational staff again have a key role to play in helping the organisation to learn about sustainability. Every organisation would love to learn how to distinguish between the ideas and opportunities that are worth pursuing, and the ones that should be left alone. Of course, it's impossible to know exactly. But they have probably already developed good instincts about which approaches will work, what kinds of partners are more valuable and trustworthy than others, and so on. And these instincts can be developed. To become more aware of what a good opportunity looks like, staff should pay attention to their gut feelings and discuss them with colleagues when new ideas, opportunities or requests come along. Try to bring individual and shared assumptions to the surface:

- What is it about this new opportunity that excites you?
- What concerns you? Are there any alarm bells and how loud are they?
- What are the potential benefits if it goes well?
- What are the risks?
- How would you describe this partner/stakeholder?

- **Take time for planning**

There's one more problem that the Yes/No Paradox causes. Often there is no time to reflect and learn before the next opportunity or project starts. The 'Study' stage of the 'Plan Do Study Act' (PDSA) cycle, or the 'Review' stage of the 'Plan Do Review' cycle, get missed.

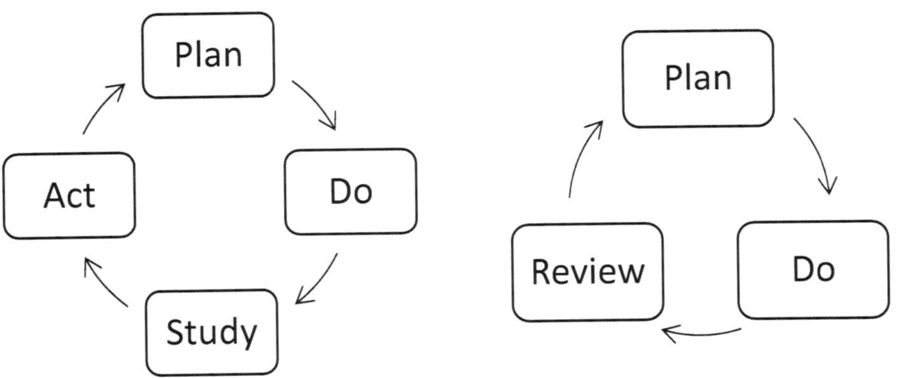

Figure 6: Two models of development cycle. In real life, 'studying' and 'reviewing' can be neglected because of delivery demands – and poor management.

Often, planning and review are skipped altogether. Who's got the time for that when there's more work to be done? Real life operating cycles look more like this:

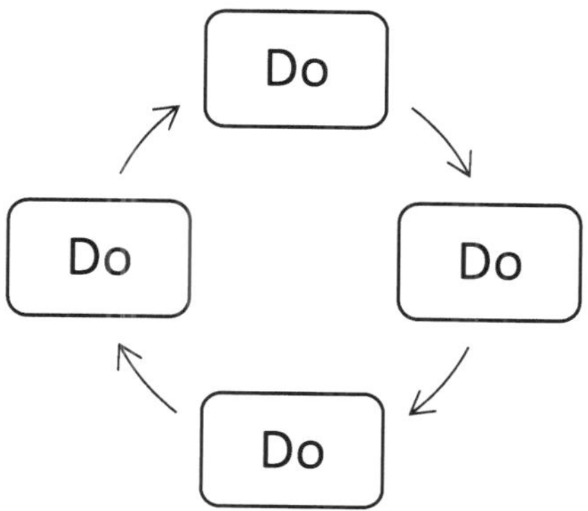

Figure 7: Real-life cycles – no development, only delivery.

As well as exhausting staff and organisational energy and resources, this is harmful to sustainability because no development takes place. Rather than learning, the same things are done over again. Time is precious and organisations need to speed up their cycles of development, but they shouldn't pretend that Figure 7 will get them anywhere but stuck in a rut.

The pressure will always be on delivery. Unlike people and issues, reflection and reporting are never going to knock urgently on the door and ask for immediate attention. Staff need to take ownership of the challenges arising from the Yes/No Paradox and step back from delivery from time to time, to reflect on and learn about their work. Not begrudgingly, and not because it has to be done, or because 'the funder is asking for this'. But because without it, organisations simply will not survive.

- **Knowing what to say 'no' to**

Staff need to learn and practice when and how to say no. As noted, this is exceptionally hard. So, ways need to be found to talk about capacity within organisations and how to manage it. Much of the pressure actually comes from internal requests within organisations – from teams, other departments, colleagues, managers, and trustees. In these circumstances, the challenge is to say no to:

- Always being available
- Resenting work

- Work controlling us
- Other people making our decisions
- Trustee or management interference
- Stress addiction
- Spreading the busyness virus.

The following ideas can be helpful for regaining control:

- Remembering organisations experience sustainability problems *because* they say 'yes' too much, not in spite of it. Taking on more will only accelerate your organisation's demise. If it dies, it can't help anyone.
- Looking back on your work to date, do you regret saying yes more than you regret saying no?
- Just because something needs to be done, does it need to be you who does it? Are you the only person who can do this? Are you the best person to be doing this?
- Busyness is not the same as progress.
- What's the opportunity cost of saying yes to this - what will it mean saying no to? Quality? Development? Breathing space? Thinking?
- 'I'm not saying no this, I'm saying yes to development, opportunities, relating, purpose, buzz and enjoyment, managing, being my best self [insert your own motivation here]...'
- 'I'm not saying no, but I'm not saying now.'
- 'If it matters to you, you'll wait, and it will be done well.'

Manage busyness and boundaries

There are many books and resources on managing time, stress and busyness, so I will just share a few tips that have made a big difference to me and people I have worked with.

- Manage your energy, not your time. If this means working when your mind is active at 3am, fine. If it means taking time off when your head isn't in it, fine. (One of the reasons there's a boom in freelancing and the 'gig economy' is that fewer and fewer people think it makes sense to expect people to be at their best only between set hours on set days).
- Set boundaries and let people know how and when you prefer to be contacted (they won't know unless you tell them).

- Turn off phone and email notifications. Such a simple, liberating thing, this really reduces stress and increases focus and productivity.
- Insist on separate equipment for work and personal use (phone, laptop etc.) and keep them separate: no work emails on personal phones – or personal time.

Reminder

The Yes/No Paradox: The things that an organisation needs to survive can also kill it. Saying 'yes' to everything is fatal.

Principle: Sustainability is about more than just money. Capacity and quality matter.

Practice: Understand when, how and what to say 'no' to.

System-level responses to the Yes/No Paradox

- Assess system and sector sustainability
- Develop pre-contract relationships and support
- Assess financial viability and reward financial stewardship

Board responses to the Yes/No Paradox

- Retain clarity of purpose
- Manage capacity

Management responses to the Yes/No Paradox

- Monitor and report on capacity
- Support staff to work within capacity
- Identify personal values – be clear on what you believe in, place value upon and are worth

Operational responses to the Yes/No Paradox

- Know what to say yes to
- Take time for planning
- Know what to say no to
- Manage busyness and boundaries

CHAPTER 7: THE EFFICIENCY PARADOX

The Efficiency Paradox: Efficiency preserves resources but can impair development.

The fourth and final paradox is that without efficiency, organisations would quickly exhaust all their energy and resources - but too much of it means they don't have the capacity to develop. They cannot innovate, be responsive – or be sustainable.

It's hard to argue against efficiency. Working efficiently makes resources go further, achieving more with less waste. Completing tasks efficiently should create more time to do other things. But when efficiency is driven by unhelpful pressures and mistaken beliefs it has limits which must be understood.

People and organisations in the non-profit sector have always had to operate very efficiently. This is partly because resources have always been tight, and partly because non-profits want their resources to reach beneficiaries and causes as fully and directly as possible. Charities that fundraise through public donations commonly publicise how many pennies in each pound donated go directly to beneficiaries, and how few on administration.

Donors, funders, commissioners and anyone else who gives money to a non-profit organisation will understandably want to know it will make a difference. They will want their monies to be converted as efficiently as possible into end results. The reality is that every business has overheads and, after 10 years of austerity, there is little extra efficiency that can be squeezed from non-profit organisations.

Pressure to reduce costs also arises from the Octopus Paradox. Organisations have resorted to developing more projects to increase turnover as funders have become less inclined to contribute to core costs and overheads. This has contributed to the reduction in size of the organisational 'centre' over the years. In extreme examples, chief officers' posts are financed through activity-based funding, requiring them to focus their time on delivery not development. Although this can seem necessary or expedient in the short-term, it should be resisted because it reduces sustainability: quality suffers; staff aren't well supported; external relationships, reputation and influence suffer; and strategy and development are forgotten.

In this context, overheads, management and administration have become dirty words in the non-profit world, like they are an extravagance rather than unavoidable costs of being in business.

There are double standards at play in the market-driven paradigm that perpetuates these pressures. I describe these below because this paradox and the myth that follows require non-profit organisations and leaders to understand and influence the policy and funding environments in which they operate.

The first double standard is about what have sometimes been portrayed as high management costs in the sector. For example, there have been several national scandals about chief officers' salaries in recent years, including some surrounding the non-profit sector. The prevailing argument in commercial firms is that high salaries are necessary to attract and retain qualified talent. In the 'voluntary' sector this doesn't apply, because voluntary should mean amateur and unpaid. It's enough to be well-meaning, why would organisations need qualified and talented leaders? The other double standard, of course, is that non-profit pay scales are generally lower than the sectors of government or media that draw attention to them. This isn't about saying non-profits are more virtuous or valuable than any other organisation. It's saying 21st century non-profit leadership is a highly specialised and demanding occupation. It's not a luxury that can be foregone or an inefficiency that can be done without.

The final double standard is that in the market-based world we live in, it is believed that diversity of supply leads to healthy competition and reduced costs. Until, that is, it comes to non-profits, where diversity of supply somehow does the opposite. If more than one organisation operates in a similar field this amounts not to healthy competition but to duplication and inefficient expense. This arises from the entirely understandable view that funders and commissioners wouldn't want to fund two organisations to do the same thing. It's also understandable that where partnerships can increase efficiency and effectiveness they should of course be pursued.

However, these views are part of the reason why it's important to stress that sustainability is not about money, sustaining organisations, or the status quo. It is about the ability to evolve within complex ecosystems. It is the *capacity* to make a lasting difference. And organisations cannot evolve, adapt or respond to complex environments if they are so efficient that they have no spare capacity. Systems need spare ('redundant') capacity in order to survive.

For example, in evolutionary biology, the presence of duplicate copies of a gene in an organism means that one copy can adapt and mutate while the duplicate is protected. Although apparently inefficient, this has been an important force in accelerating evolution. Similarly, in the human body, having two eyes and ears means that even if one is injured we can still see and hear. In engineering, redundancy means building things with more capacity and greater tolerance than they actually need. For example, for safety reasons bridges are designed to be able to carry more weight than they will normally need to.

Other examples of redundant capacity that supports sustainability include:

- Back-up systems (like spare electricity generators in hospitals; computer back-ups; off-site records archives etc.)
- Performance monitoring systems (like quality assurance systems; evaluation processes; staff appraisals etc.)
- Spare or 'slack' resources (like farmers' use of fallow fields to ensure healthy crop rotation; organisations having spare floor space to accommodate hot-desks or new recruits etc.).

As a reminder, these are good, effective, desirable *inefficient* things! If they are cut, organisations may save money in the short-term – but they will be less sustainable in the longer term. They will not have the capacity to make a lasting difference.

Other organisational examples of redundant capacity supporting sustainability include:

In planning, redundant capacity would include not completely filling workplans and calendars at the start of the year, ensuring there is some slack so that interesting opportunities can be pursued as they arise. Organisations may use an idea screening matrix so that staff aren't so busy with 'more of the same' delivery that they miss opportunities to respond to exciting ventures that could take the organisation in new directions.

In human resource terms, redundant capacity would include things like time for staff to take part in meetings, attend training, shadow colleagues, work on developments and have time to think.

In financial terms, it includes budgeting for contingencies. For example, payroll costs might sensibly be estimated at 120% of actual costs to allow for contingencies like maternity cover, recruitment costs, hiring temporary staff to cover vacant posts and so on.

Organisations cannot evolve, adapt or respond to complex environments if they are so efficient that they have no spare capacity.

Redundant capacity is a critical part of sustainability, because it enables organisations to adapt and change.

A further paradox of efficiency: The chicken or the egg?
How do organisations increase their capacity when they have limited capacity? A familiar example of this 'chicken and egg' paradox is when a manager needs to recruit a new member of staff. The manager is so busy coping with the gaps caused by the vacant position that they don't have time to get around to

recruiting. If they had time to recruit, the new staff member would take over and the manager would have more time.

In some cases, resources will be needed before the capacity can be developed. In the recruitment example, the manager would need money in the budget before being able to employ a new worker. This would seem a logical way to proceed. At the same time, until the manager frees some capacity by saying 'no' to some of the operational demands that take time and attention away from recruitment, nothing will happen.

Organisations are sometimes frozen into inaction because they cannot reconcile the chicken and egg of capacity and resources. Neither comes first, they are part of a cycle that can only be broken by investing in spare capacity. Spare capacity somewhere in the system lets organisations cope with being overstretched, or even overwhelmed, for a short time until their resources catch up.
In sustainability challenges like this, organisations typically have to take both approaches – bring in new resources that will eventually generate more capacity, but in the short-term create free capacity by not doing something else. If organisations have spare capacity, the challenge is easier to manage. But if they are operating at full efficiency, it requires them to be able to stop, or at least pause, some of what they are doing, something that requires clear understanding and support at all levels.

Overview – the Paradox in brief

The Efficiency Paradox: Efficiency preserves resources but can impair development.

Principle: Organisations cannot evolve, adapt or respond without spare capacity.

Practice: Balance strategy and scrutiny. Invest in capacity building.

System-level responses to the Efficiency Paradox

- **Balance strategy and scrutiny**

Sustainability in the policy and funding environment is based on developing relationships of trust, working with others to design programmes and discover solutions. Commissioners and policy makers don't and can't know all of the right answers to all of the right questions. Once we accept this, we can begin to let go of the illusion of certainty and control. We can design strategies, policies and funding programmes that release non-profit organisations' creativity and commitment by releasing them from the constraints of monitoring, compliance and attribution.

Naturally, we still need to know that work is being done safely, effectively, and to a high standard. But we can, and must, do this without dictating outcomes, activities and performance standards because:

- **We're not close or clever enough.** Funders and policy makers are usually at least two steps removed from the worlds they are trying to influence. They are unlikely to have the insight or information to know what will work in a complex environment that they are *part of but can't control.*
- **KPIs are ineffective.** Key Performance Indicators typically measure the wrong thing, focusing on process as a proxy for outcomes and effectiveness: how many things will be done, with how many people, by when? They overlook outcomes in favour of what is easy to measure.
- **Performance targets skew behaviour.** Holding people to account for targets generates mutual distrust. And it skews behaviour, so that instead of focusing on achieving the outcome, people focus on the measure. For instance, to achieve targets relating to waiting times, doctors' surgeries have adopted the practice of refusing advance appointments for patients. Instead, patients must phone every morning to request an appointment for the same day. Because of the volume of people calling the surgery at the same time, it can take a patient several days to get through. But these days are invisible, not appearing on any waiting time statistics. Doctors have successfully gamed the system, creating the illusion of efficiency and effectiveness. Any other organisation or team will do the same thing in similar circumstances. At best, this will be in a spirit of *'Let's give them the targets they want, then we can get on with our real work'*. At worst, it leads to satisficing, a form of malicious compliance where people do exactly what has been asked – and no more. This

is not sustainable in a policy and funding environment where we need not only data, but reliable intelligence about what it means.

The biggest leadership challenge of our time is to move from understanding that power must be devolved, to discovering ways to do this effectively.

Once leaders accept that they aren't in control, they can learn to become enablers and facilitators. When confronting the Efficiency Paradox, funders and policy makers can facilitate conversations with non-profit organisations about what high-quality, efficient performance looks like. They can enable exploration and risk-taking, designing clear strategies which leave room for responsiveness and evolution.

- **Support capacity building**

If the Change Paradox requires evolution, and evolution is impossible without spare capacity, system-level actors must support capacity building. They must tolerate the existence of slack within the system. For instance, funders should make more of their funding 'unrestricted', free of performance targets and not bounded by narrow project parameters. This encourages non-profit organisations to operate flexibly, adapting their operating models in response to emerging evidence, needs and trends. It allows financial reserves to be accumulated by organisations that operate effectively. It also builds knowledge reserves: providing resources, time and money for staff training, learning and development.

Reflection: How comfortable are you with these ideas?

It is knowledge not money that is the real lifeblood of most non-profit organisations. They need to know what matters to beneficiaries and other stakeholders; have evidence of need; be able to scan the horizon for new threats and opportunities; have technical expertise; and be up to date with the latest evidence, policy, legislation and regulatory requirements. So, funders and policy makers should ensure that the workforce within their sectors has adequate access to training, learning and development opportunities.

- **Support innovation and responsiveness**

Design innovative programmes e.g. collaborative commissioning models, partnerships with other investors and policy makers to find answers to emerging needs.

Mandate proper innovation, not the façade of requiring organisations to develop new projects in response to a funding or tendering opportunity. Rather, use funding as a form of action research. Set challenges to be explored, based on the knotty questions and 'wicked' challenges you and your communities face. This will resemble Victorian-era sponsorship of scientific exploration, with funding, incentives and prizes being awarded for projects that find breakthrough solutions to previously intractable problems.

If necessary, create separate funds for innovation, development and challenge, with looser criteria and more freedom than might normally be expected. This can create space for creativity by freeing up the new fund from some of the constraints your other funds and processes might have.

This approach requires investment in evaluation, which must be built into project budgets. Scotland Funders' Forum makes the observation that between 5-8% of project time and budgets are spent on self-evaluation. That might sound manageable and acceptable, but it's the equivalent of a day a month for a full-time member of staff. Evaluation and learning are important and need to be supported with adequate resources.

- **Welcome deviation**

If we are to solve currently intractable problems and manage ever-dwindling resources, we must welcome curiosity, exploration and deviation. Medieval royal courts realised that they would learn nothing from acolytes and hangers-on, so they employed court jesters and gave them licence to disrupt, challenge and provoke. Commissioners and policy makers need to find and work with people who are prepared to say 'no' and who can point out when they are asking the wrong questions or addressing the wrong problem. Innovators, provocateurs and mavericks are not always easy to work with and deviation is not always welcome. But any and all insights must be welcomed if we are to navigate our way out of our current and unsustainable ways of thinking and acting.

- **Facilitate collaboration**

It is not unusual for commissioners who use competitive tendering to bemoan the lack of collaboration between the organisations they fund. This is a bit like sitting in a car complaining about traffic: we are part of the problem we would like to solve.

System-level interventions can encourage innovation by creating the conditions for, and facilitating, collaboration. Commissioners can play important roles in facilitating collaboration, for example hosting networks, learning events, and collaborative commissioning processes. Even if they are unable to fund collaboration they should not take it for granted. To date, many Public Social Partnerships in the UK have relied on the goodwill of providers to commit unpaid time to the process of developing new service models and partnerships[1]. This goodwill tends not to be sustained if the resulting model is then put out to competitive tender. Similarly, commissioners who expect to take providers' proprietary service models and share them (or put them up for tender) are unlikely to be rewarded with more collaboration in future. If the reward for innovation and developing intellectual property is to have it taken away, organisations will not volunteer it for long.

- **Avoid the inefficiency of short-term funding**

It is inefficient to fund for short timescales because of the time and expense involved in setting up services, systems and staffing before outcomes can be achieved. Funding cycles of 1-2 years are disproportionately costly and inefficient. This isn't to say things should be open-ended or lack urgency. Evidence and experience tell us that creativity benefits from having constraints to work within and push against (e.g. sonnets and haiku have strict formal constraints within which creativity can flourish. Pressure on time and resources can also accelerate innovation). If short-term funding cycles must be used, they should be used to gather evidence for further development.

- **Attend to the negative effects of competition and tendering**

The main purpose of competitive tendering is to reduce price by increasing competition. Until quite recently, it was arguably achieving these goals. However, this is changing rapidly. Firstly, evidence shows that an increasing number of organisations are declining to submit tenders for contracts that they will be expected to subsidise. And secondly, examples are emerging of third-sector partnerships, involving some of the biggest players, being founded on agreements between providers to no longer compete with one another.

---

[1] Public Social Partnerships are collaborative commissioning models where services are co-designed by commissioners, communities and service providers.

Commissioners who wish to address the Efficiency Paradox should expect non-profit organisations to recover the full costs of delivering services. High-profile cases such as the repeated failure of the East Coast mainline train franchise and the collapse of Carillion[2] provide ample evidence of the risks to policy makers – and public monies – of pursuing the lowest cost option. No sensible tendering exercise would fail to provide enough slack for contingencies. Low-cost tenders and services should be assessed critically. Do underpriced tenders over-promise on delivery and outcomes? What is being sacrificed to achieve lower costs than comparable applications: Quality? Capacity? Safety? Staff terms and conditions? If these things matter, many organisations are already working well beyond sustainable levels.

In Scotland, where this book was written, the 2014 Sustainable Procurement Duty requires commissioners to consider how to facilitate the involvement of small and medium enterprises, third sector bodies and supported businesses. One way to achieve this is to offer contracts in smaller 'lots' to allow smaller companies to bid. It may be less efficient than awarding contracts to one large provider: but it's more sustainable. It reduces the risk of market failure, being held to ransom by 'too big to fail' contractors and promotes market diversity.

Board responses to the Efficiency Paradox

- **Balance scrutiny and strategy**

One of the most important, and easiest, things any board can do to address the Efficiency Paradox is to work out how much of its time and attention is given to scrutiny, and how much to strategy. 'Scrutiny' is made up of activities that focus attention *in, down* and *back*. Things like:

- Poring over spreadsheets looking only for budget overspend.
- Reading reports and discussing only those things that have not been achieved.
- Debating Key Performance Indicators but losing focus on what they mean.

Strategy on the other hand is about looking outwards, up and ahead. Things like:

- Exploring scenarios and the outcomes of different strategies and choices.

[2] Carillion was Britain's second largest construction firm but collapsed with debts of around £1bn, with nearly the same amount of deficit in its pension fund.

- Identifying trends and projecting them into the future.
- Discussing the strategic plan and progress being made towards it.
- Updating the plan based on learning, emerging trends and new goals.

Of course, this is about balance. To do their jobs properly, trustees must give their attention to both scrutiny and strategy.

- **Exercise financial oversight**

Trustees should look out for underspent budget lines, as they often contain warning signs about where so-called 'efficiency savings' are being made. For example, if staffing budgets are underspent, this can be a sign that the organisation has vacant posts or that it is working 'efficiently', because existing staff are covering work that would have been done by the vacant postholder. But this is likely to mean staff are working to full capacity and are probably not taking (or being given) time to develop their roles or their skills. Long term this is unsustainable because if training budgets are underspent the organisation is not developing its capabilities for the future as well as it could. People are usually motivated by learning new things and by developing new initiatives, so if they don't have these opportunities in your organisation they may seek them elsewhere. Worse still, they could stay with you but lose that motivation, becoming passive and withdrawing effort and goodwill. It's also unsustainable because the organisation won't develop and will get left behind in a changing world (the Change Paradox).

- **Beware of false economies**

If the board is having to consider budget cuts, beware of making false economies. Seemingly small changes can have disproportionate impacts on staff morale and hamstring the organisation's capacity for survival. It is well accepted that factors like pay, annual leave, sickness entitlements do not increase motivation. But they are 'hygiene factors' - minimum requirements whose absence or loss is demotivating. Seek staff input about where savings can be made without affecting capacity and morale. Organisations that do this are often surprised by the effort staff will put in and the ideas they come up with.

- **Make remuneration decisions with sustainability in mind**

Remuneration is a vexatious issue, particularly for senior staff salaries, for whom it is often hard to find comparable benchmarks. Whatever decision is taken, remember the right decision isn't always the easy one and that strong leadership is required. Non-profit organisations sometimes try to skirt around sustainability challenges by making temporary salary arrangements. In some cases, these are justified. For example, boards might withhold a decision about an annual pay increase until they know how finances are developing during the year. In other cases, decisions can be fudged. For example, boards sometimes decide to manage cuts by reducing salaries or working hours across the whole organisation. This sounds controversial, but in the cases where I have seen it happen, staff have preferred it (or even offered it as a suggestion) to the alternative – redundancies or project closures. The strategic rationale (or hope) is that people or posts are not lost, the capacity to regrow is sustained, and the organisation buys itself some time to weather the storm. However, this approach typically only delays the inevitable – the need to restructure for the longer term, with hard decisions to make about strategies, finances and redundancies.

As with the Octopus Paradox, in these cases posts, activities and functions that support organisational learning and development should be retained wherever possible. In this way, the organisation retains key knowledge and capabilities for future regrowth.

Indeed, one of the ways to manage sustainability challenges is to think of the organisation like an accordion or concertina. There are times when it will need to grow, expanding outwards in response to demand and resources. There are other times when it will need to shrink, losing resources because money is tight. Neither stage is easy and they both place strain on the organisation and its people. But, like it or not, this is often the key to sustainability for non-profit organisations. Growth is not always possible (or sometimes even desirable), and the prospect of decline is never far away.

- **Assess and prioritise organisational capacity**

Each of the areas of action above can be summed up simply: to address the sustainability paradoxes, boards must assess and prioritise organisational capacity.

In terms of the Efficiency Paradox, the assessment, which should be conducted with managers, might include metrics like:

- Board time spent in 'scrutiny' and 'strategy'.
- Budgets and expenditure for staffing, training and development.
- The level and use of resources (including money and staff, but also knowledge, IT, premises etc.) Are they being used efficiently and effectively in pursuit of the organisation's goals?
- Staffing: staff level, turnover, vacancies, satisfaction.
- The number and nature of innovations and developments.
- The number and nature of knowledge creating opportunities (e.g. participation in networks, partnerships, pilot projects).
- Agreeing and monitoring the proportion of time staff spend 'on task' (delivery) and how much on building capacity (development).

Management responses to the Efficiency Paradox

- **Review costs and ways of working**

It is important for non-profit sustainability that managers review costs regularly. This includes looking critically at their organisations' ways of working, from the organisational structure to models of delivery and working methods. To be sustainable, these all need to be as efficient and effective as possible. But not too efficient - it's perfectly possible for organisations to be so efficient that they become ineffective. So, rather than asking whether every activity 'adds value' for customers and end users (an approach used in the commercial world to strip away unnecessary activity), ask whether every activity adds value to sustainability. This can help to protect those valuable areas of 'redundant capacity' described above.

Reviewing costs also ensures the true costs of work are understood. This is vital for ensuring funding applications cover the full costs of delivery and it helps demonstrate efficiency and value for money to donors and funders.

Is your organisation doing the right things in the right ways? Is it the right organisation to be doing this particular piece of work? Does the work really need to be done? And if so, does it really need to be your organisation that does it?

- **Increase the slack, reduce the stress**

Managers should build slack into budgets, tenders and funding applications for contingencies. No sensible budget would be made without allowing for unexpected expenses. This carries over into line management of staff too – time and allowance need to be given for tasks that can seem unproductive, like administration, planning, communication, practice sharing and so on. This isn't to say that managers should accept inefficiency, but that they should have a clear sense of the activities that are necessary for work to be done well.

Similarly, managers must support their teams to manage the paradox by, for example, allocating time for communication, helping to protect development time, ensuring holiday and training entitlements are fully used, and being alert to the signs of overwork and stress. Encourage and normalise conversations about workloads, stress and healthy working practices. Keep an open door and an open mind.

- **Educate others about sustainability**

When talking about sustainability, particularly to funders, managers should talk about working more effectively and having the capacity to make a lasting difference. It's about long-term impact, not (just) money. Managers should encourage honest conversations about if and how their organisations can do things differently and make it clear if they are, or are not, asking for more money.

- **Manage capacity**

Managers must accurately appraise how much capacity their staff and teams have - and recognise when it is overloaded. Staff wellbeing has risen in prominence as an indicator of organisational sustainability over the last few years. People and teams are struggling to meet increased demand with fewer resources. They wrestle the Octopus daily and know all about the Yes/No Paradox. Managers should support staff to deal with excessive pressures and workloads, particularly before generating or permitting new developments. Remember that the most valuable staff usually find job satisfaction in developing new initiatives, so it may be better to remove existing burdens rather than forbidding involvement in new opportunities.

Operational responses to the Efficiency Paradox

- **Practise self-care and care for others**

Like managers, individual staff need to recognise their own capacity and when it is overloaded. This is not easy, as stress - and stress related illnesses - are insidious. They creep up on us slowly and we sometimes don't realise we're affected until long after they have taken hold. Individual sustainability is a crucial part of organisational sustainability. If we care about our organisations and the people we serve, it is imperative that we take good care of ourselves and our colleagues.

- **Enjoy downtime**

People who work in the non-profit world need breaks as much as anyone else, but they often feel guilty for taking time away from being of service to the people or causes that drive them. So, lunch breaks are not taken, or they are taken at people's desks where they can feel useful, ignoring the tiredness and lack of productivity that inevitably follow later. Similarly, people's dedication to their work; guilt at taking time away from it; or misplaced sense of indispensability; mean that entitlements to holidays and 'time off in lieu' might not be taken. Again, it isn't always easy to take breaks and time off, particularly when people experience (or internalise) pressure to work at maximum efficiency, or when it feels like 24 hours a day aren't enough to make the impact they want to have. But downtime and breaks help to sustain our energy and enable us to work more effectively. Even the most efficient organisms and the most indispensable machines need downtime and maintenance. Humans are no different. Research and experience show us that taking time away from tasks increases productivity and creativity. Even the most driven and committed people need to find ways to take and enjoy time off.

- **Protect development time**

No matter how much encouragement is given by managers or trustees, if operational staff don't set aside and protect time for developing new ideas and opportunities, it won't happen. As we saw with the Yes/No Paradox, delivery is always going to seem like a more urgent – and efficient – use of time. But allocating, protecting and taking time for development will increase job satisfaction and effectiveness and, ultimately, improve efficiency.

- **Highlight inefficiencies and false economies**

In any organisation, operational staff are the ones most likely to experience the inefficiencies built into work processes, funding requirements, reporting systems etc. Ironically, these are often designed to increase efficiency, so staff have a duty to address or raise them. Of course, this will be more welcome and possible in some organisations that others. In sustainable ones, voices calling out about inefficiency and false economies will be heard.

Reminder

The Efficiency Paradox: Efficiency preserves resources but can impair development.

Principle: Organisations cannot evolve, adapt or respond without spare capacity.

Practice: Balance strategy and scrutiny. Invest in capacity building.

System-level responses to the Efficiency Paradox

- Balance strategy and scrutiny
- Support capacity building
- Support innovation and responsiveness
- Welcome deviation
- Facilitate collaboration
- Avoid the inefficiency of short-term funding
- Attend to the negative effects of competition and tendering

Board responses to the Efficiency Paradox

- Balance scrutiny and strategy
- Exercise financial oversight
- Beware of false economies
- Make remuneration decisions with sustainability in mind
- Assess and prioritise organisational capacity

Management responses to the Efficiency Paradox

- Review costs and ways of working
- Increase the slack
- Educate others about sustainability
- Manage capacity

Operational responses to the Efficiency Paradox

- Recognise individual and team capacity
- Practise self-care and care for others

- Enjoy downtime
- Protect development time
- Highlight inefficiencies and false economies

CHAPTER 8: THE MYTH OF PERPETUAL MOTION

The myth of perpetual motion: The belief that work can continue without replenishing inputs

We conclude this section not with another paradox but with a myth: the Myth of Perpetual Motion. This is the mistaken belief that organisations can somehow keep going once funding stops. It also manifests as a belief that momentum can be sustained after an initial push. For example, organisations often publish a strategic plan and believe that will be enough to unite staff and stakeholders behind a new vision. Sustaining momentum is impossible without further impetus. The perpetual motion machine has not been invented: nothing is self-sustaining.

Funders perpetuate the Myth when they ask applicants how work will be sustained once funding comes to an end. This question is understandable insofar as funders try not to create dependency on their funds. It is not sustainable for projects to return to the same pot time after time, and not just because the pot is limited. Things change, and projects need to adapt and learn in response. However, the expectation that projects can be sustained once the funding stops must be understood as a dangerous myth. It's a bit like the famous scene from the 1980s television series *Mork and Mindy* where Mork (the naive newcomer to planet Earth played by Robin Williams) tosses an egg into the air, seeing the potential of the unborn chick within to 'Fly, be free!'. Inevitably, the outcome is not good. Organisations can and do fly, but they need time to develop, and we can't expect one- or two-years' funding to 'pump prime' them to go it alone. They will always need income and resources from somewhere.

Exit strategies and sustaining impact

Because sustainability is about impact not just organisations, funders could rightly argue that they are investing in the organisation's capacity to make a lasting difference, and that once funding stops the impact can be sustained. This is indeed possible. People and communities can develop capacity and do things independently. For example, a funder might support physical activity groups to encourage inactive people to exercise more. After a while, people in the groups might get to know each other so well that they become more of a social group. Although these still achieve outcomes, like maintaining physical activity and increasing community connections, the groups are no longer physical activity groups for inactive people. In these cases, the funder has built participants' capacity to shape and run their own activities. It has made a lasting difference (sustained levels of activity), and it might therefore support the group to go its own way. The group might set up as an independent body, for example registering as a charity in its own right, or simply remain an informal group of friends having fun together. But it will still need inputs of some kind: venues, equipment, food and drink, volunteer time, simple administration like keeping a register of people's contact details. It will not be self-sustaining – nothing is.

Similarly, an organisation might make a lasting difference by encouraging its projects or issues to be mainstreamed, adopted by other organisations so that special services aren't needed any more. Organisations that promote equality issues are a good example of this is. At one time, equalities organisations had to focus on educating other organisations about what would now be seen as fairly basic messages about racial awareness and equality. These messages have been accepted and adopted in the cultural mainstream, to the extent that racial equality is part of everyone's business, not a specialist subject. Other examples include the trade union movement's influence on safe working practices and the environmental movement's success in mainstreaming recycling.

Once success has been achieved at a policy or societal level, and embedded in cultural or organisational life, a lasting difference has been made. Messages and behaviours will have been mainstreamed, they will be adopted, owned and spread further by other people. But again, it is not self-sustaining. For example, inequalities and discrimination still exist, workplace abuses of health and safety laws still take place, and even if recycling were universally practised, it is only part of wider, more entrenched practices relating to consumption, waste and environmental sustainability.

At the very least, messages need to retain prominence in people's consciousness or they risk being lost over time. This needs some form of resource like information materials; people to keep websites and promotional materials up to date; someone to keep campaigns in the public awareness. For example, messages about safe sex, HIV, AIDS and sexually transmitted diseases (STDs) were amongst the most prominent of the 1980s but have had less prominence in the lives of young people growing up in the 1990s and 2000s. Seeing current news stories about the increase of STDs would surprise people who grew up in the 1980s who might have thought the job of education was done.

We need to challenge the myth of self-sustaining organisations and impacts. Nothing in the known universe is self-sustaining. There's a reason why the perpetual motion machine hasn't been invented. Nothing can run forever without some kind of input from or exchange with its environment.

Overview - the Myth in Brief

The Myth of Perpetual Motion: Work can continue without inputs being replenished.

Principle: Sustainability does not mean self-sustaining.

Practice: Prepare for funding to end. Invest in capacity building.

System-level responses to the Myth of Perpetual Motion

- **Accept system flux and adjust to system lifecycles**

System actors understand the Change Paradox and recognise that as a population's needs and resources change over time, so must the policies and approaches that are developed in response. This comes with a need to accept – and to help others accept – that policy and funding cycles will end. Equally, systems are always evolving, so it is important to remember that the end of one cycle is the beginning of another. System actors must become aware of the different lifecycle stages that populations, systems, policy-making, funding, organisations and communities are in, and adjust their plans, responses and communications accordingly.

- **Understand and explain your approach to sustainability**

Early in the funding cycle funders should support organisations to prepare plans for when the funding ends. This means more than asking the question *'How will this work be sustained after the life of the funding?'*. As we have seen, this has no easy answer, and maybe no answer at all. Instead, funders should identify what sustainability means for themselves first:

- What do you believe sustainability to be, in your context? (Is it about impact, organisations, or both? Is it about organisational survival? Money? Or more?)
- What would sustainable funding look like?
- Where does your money come from? How sustainable is this?
- Where does it go? Which types of organisations get it? How does it reach them (e.g. by application, competitive tender, or invitation)?
- What are the funding practices that support sustainability – and what are the ones that diminish it (e.g. application and reporting systems, length of funding, capacity-building support)?
- What do you want the legacy of funding to be? (Results? Outputs? Outcomes? Learning? Capacity?)
- How prepared are you to support other organisations to understand and take action on sustainability?

- **Engage communities and stakeholders**

System actors can either enable stakeholders by sharing information about, and responsibility for, system sustainability – or disable them by making them passive recipients of decisions and actions. The former may seem riskier – more informed and engaged communities of stakeholders might not make life easier for policy makers or funders. But disengaged, passive stakeholders can be more dangerous still, and not just when they mobilise and rise up against the architects of the system that has marginalised them. Enlightened policy makers and funders realise the benefits of proactively seeking the involvement of their stakeholders. With a better understanding of a population's needs and resources, policy makers, funders and others can work with stakeholders to design better systems. When people themselves have identified the need to change, the closure of outdated services or the arrival of new models meet with less resistance. Innovative ideas and community-led solutions can emerge, reducing reliance on services and increasing ownership of processes and outcomes.

- **Model sustainable practices**

Funders should share their understanding of sustainability with the organisations they support and embody it in their practices. For example, sustainability should be defined, and expectations should be explained, before funding is awarded. If funders expect long-term outcomes, they should provide long-term funding. Otherwise, they should agree proportionate outcomes (and measurement/reporting processes) with organisations. Post-award, funders can provide information, support or training to help organisations to understand the paradoxes and develop the sustainability capabilities. (The Lasting Difference resource, available as a free download for non-commercial use, is designed to help facilitate these conversations.)

Board responses to the Myth of Perpetual Motion

- **Identify what to sustain**

Trustees have an important role to play in identifying what the organisation should seek to sustain. As the Change Paradox identifies, things change, and things end. But something at the core of the organisation will persist over time while other things change around it. Trustees are the guardians of this core, helping to preserve and sustain what really matters. However, as the people directing the organisation, they must also preserve the necessary distance and discipline to be prepared to let other things go. At some point in a board's life, hard decisions will almost certainly need to be taken about projects, areas of work or commitments which cannot be sustained.

Trustees should agree criteria for making these decisions, for example: if goals have been achieved, needs have been met, costs are not being recovered or the activity is no longer strategically important. They should encourage exit strategies to be developed for new and existing commitments, again rooted in identifying and preserving the organisation's core.

- **Provide visible backing**

Boards need to provide backing for their management teams. For example, managers need to know how far they can go in pushing back against funders' expectations of, or belief in, the Myth of Perpetual Motion. Board backing might have to be more visible than usual, for example with the Chair or nominated representative being prepared to advocate on the organisation's behalf, or work alongside management, during contract negotiations.

- **Share understanding of sustainability**

Trustees should also agree their own understanding of sustainability, making sure they are not perpetuating the Myth of Perpetual Motion, for example by expecting more work for less money, or expecting every aspect of their organisation's work to continue indefinitely.

Management responses to the Myth of Perpetual Motion

- **Look to the horizon**

Managers should always have one eye on the horizon beyond the current funding cycle. Exit strategies should be built in at an early stage. Whether the strategy is to mainstream a piece of work, seek more funding, or discontinue it, contingencies should be planned for. (See Chapters 18-20 on Exit Strategies).

- **Challenge the myth**

When there are challenges with sustaining activity and impact, managers should raise these with funders. Managers need to confidently challenge the Myth when they encounter it. This might mean a number of things. For example, when a funding application asks how the work will be sustained, managers can give the usual pat answer about seeking funding from other sources. But they can also explain their approach to sustainability – and how they will develop the capacity to make a lasting difference. Similarly, if a funder expects long-term outcomes to be achieved with short-term funding, managers should point this out and offer suggestions for achievable contributions the organisation can make in the available timescale.

- **Sustain momentum**

The Myth applies just as much to internal forces as it does to external. Common examples of this are when managers invest time and expense in developing strategies but overlook the importance of implementing them, or when change programmes fail. Managers should not assume that because they have communicated something it has been understood, or that because a strategy has been given an initial push, it will gather momentum like a snowball rolling downhill. They need to sustain the momentum behind strategies, programmes and communications, particularly when the early signs of change are visible. To be sustainable, changes and strategies need to be fully embedded in systems and ways of working, and momentum should be maintained until this is achieved.

Operational responses to the Myth of Perpetual Motion

The ability to combat the Myth of Perpetual Motion is quite limited for operational staff. However, they may have very important roles to play in building capacity. It is frontline staff who will most likely spot the signs of issues becoming mainstreamed, groups becoming self-organising and individuals becoming self-resilient. They should highlight this to the people involved, who may not realise how far they have come, and to managers who can help manage the transition to the next level of development.

They should take pride in these achievements and resist the temptation to do anything other than encourage further independence. This isn't always easy. As noted elsewhere, we like to be needed, and if we're honest our jobs depend on it. But in the same way a parent can be both heartbroken and proud when their child grows up and leaves the nest, staff should be proud when they are no longer needed. This isn't to say they will or should be out of work. Again, working with managers, staff can help to identify the next area of need or development and make the transition to that in a structured way.

Reminder

The Myth of Perpetual Motion: Work can continue without inputs being replenished.

Principle: Sustainability does not mean self-sustaining.

Practice: Prepare for funding to end. Invest in capacity building.

System-level responses to the Myth of Perpetual Motion

- Accept system flux and adjust to system lifecycles
- Understand and explain your approach to sustainability
- Engage communities and stakeholders
- Model sustainable practices
- Do something about sustainability or stop talking about it

Board responses to the Myth of Perpetual Motion

- Identify what to sustain
- Provide visible backing to management
- Share understanding of sustainability

Management responses to the Myth of Perpetual Motion

- Look to the horizon beyond the current funding cycle and identify exit strategies
- Challenge the myth

Operational responses to the Myth of Perpetual Motion

- Look for the signs of self-organising groups and self-resilient individuals
- Encourage independence
- Work with managers on identified exit strategies

CHAPTER 9: ASSESSING CAPACITY

Two recurring aspects within each of the Sustainability Paradoxes are budgets and capacity. Before we summarise the Paradoxes, this matrix and the descriptions below set out different scenarios that occur in relation to budgets and capacity. They can be used to assess an organisation's position – and take action on it.

		Budget	
		Over	**Below**
Capacity	**Over**	**Shipwreck** **Action:** • Control spending • Downsize • Restructure **Stakeholder strategy:** Enlist	**Octopus** **Action:** • Retract and align tentacles • Focus **Stakeholder strategy:** Manage
	Below	**Pirate** **Action:** • Financial control and management • Cut costs **Stakeholder strategy:** Parlay (invest) and Parley (negotiate)	**Cruiser** **Action:** • Monitor and review • Invest and develop **Stakeholder strategy:** Involve

Figure 8: Actions and stakeholder strategies for managing capacity and resources

Over budget, over capacity: Shipwreck

Description

It might not be shipwrecked yet, but the organisation is heading for the rocks at full throttle. It might be over budget because of poor planning or financial control, or because staff are working above capacity. It might be undercharging for its work or underestimating its true costs. The organisation has possibly had to respond to unexpectedly high levels of demand (incurring direct costs like staffing, project resources etc.), and/or taken on things it should have said no to. This is an unsustainable position. Quality, safety and staff wellbeing are at risk, as is the organisation's reputation (at best) and its future (at worst).

Action: Control spending, downsize, restructure.

Urgent action is needed to steer the ship away from the rocks. Seeking emergency funding might help to 'bail out' the ship but this may take more time than the organisation has. In the short-term, spending needs to be brought back under control, which means reviewing commitments including possibly stopping some areas of activity if required. If extra funding (and the capacity it brings) isn't found, the organisation will need to downsize and restructure. Crucially, new plans and controls will be needed to avoid repeating the situation in future.

Stakeholder strategy: Enlist

Enlisting stakeholder support is essential. Stakeholders, both internal (e.g. staff, clients, volunteers) and external (e.g. referrers, funders, partners, communities) will want to understand what has happened and why. Honest engagement is needed to enlist their support in sustaining the organisation. Can they help with capacity? Can they help with funding? Are they prepared to give the organisation time to turn things around?

Over budget, below capacity: Pirate

Description

This organisation has overspent its budget but has capacity to spare, which could indicate a number of things. It may be that it has invested in infrastructure (staffing, premises, IT etc.) but the work hasn't developed as planned (e.g. partnerships might still be developing, referrals might be awaited). There might be poor financial management and control. Or it may be carrying too many staff and unnecessary overheads.

Action: Control finances, cut costs. Use spare capacity or lose it.
Financial control is needed. A plan should be developed for bringing finances and capacity back into line with each other. Budgets and structures should be reviewed to find savings and costs should be cut accordingly. Spare capacity that has already been paid for can be put to use to generate income (e.g. hiring out under-used premises or resources; assigning staff to developing business and generating income).

Stakeholder strategy: Parlay/Parley
Two similar words with different meanings are useful here. The first, parlay, means to invest or gamble profitably. The pirate has spent money and accumulated resources but it remains to be seen if, or maybe how, the investment will pay off. Stakeholders could feel they have been robbed by the pirate and want to know where the treasure is buried.

So, 'parley' is required: a word from pirate folklore, meaning to talk and negotiate. Organisations in this situation should ask stakeholders for a parley, negotiating to show they are trustworthy and, if necessary, can change their ways. Are investors and donors happy for the pirate to have spare capacity? Maybe they are glad that this ensures a healthy level of quality, safety and insurance against future risks. Or do they want to see more for their money? Are beneficiaries feeling let down by a lack of service, or are they getting a very high-quality service that makes up for it? How will they feel if this changes, for example if the service gets stretched more thinly when demand increases, or if it gets cut to bring finances under control? The sustainability of piracy as an occupation will depend on the answers to these questions. But it's a questionable strategy for a non-profit organisation.

Below budget, over capacity: Octopus

Description
Financially, this organisation is working within its means. But it has over-committed in terms of capacity, appearing to have taken too much on. This might be short-term – the octopus might recently have used its tentacles to bring in extra resources to increase capacity, but these have yet to be deployed. It might have a frugal financial controller who doesn't want to release money for extra capacity, letting the burden be carried by staff or services elsewhere. It may have a prudent strategy of saving to invest in a new direction or development. But its ability to attend to this could be hampered by having spread its tentacles in too many directions.

Action: Retract and align tentacles. Focus.

The octopus is possibly engaged in a successful strategy but needs to assign its spare resources to increase its capacity or retract one or more of its tentacles. Either way, in the short-term it should recognise and deal with organisational overload before growing new tentacles. Longer term, it should focus on the direction it wants to go in and ensure its tentacles are aligned with this – and with each other.

Stakeholder strategy: Manage

Involving funders, partners and beneficiaries effectively is one of the core Sustainability Capabilities for a good reason (see Part 3). Stakeholder involvement can provide intelligence and insight to help the organisation adapt. But if the octopus has been pulled out of shape by stakeholder expectations, it should make sure it manages these effectively. This requires honest conversations about the limits and strains on capacity and the way that stakeholders affect – or could be affected by – this.

Below budget, below capacity: Cruiser

Description

With capacity and budget to spare, this organisation can take time to explore the world around it. It can invest in new developments. Having healthy capacity and budgets should be signs of a well-run organisation. It is also possible that cruisers are in the early stages of development, or indeed that they are not yet clear on, or are losing sight of, their purpose. This situation can arise when, for example, an organisation is created (or receives an injection of income) in response to a new government policy.

However, with the risk of being an organisation in search of a purpose, the cruiser could drift off course. Research shows that organisations and people are at their most innovative when they are under some pressure to perform (technological advancements during wartime are an oft-cited example). So purposeful exploration is the key. It is unlikely any organisation can cruise for long, so time spent in this quadrant is to be appreciated but not squandered.

Action: Monitor and review, invest and develop

Working within budget and with spare capacity should be signs of organisational health. Cruisers should monitor and review their situation to reassure themselves and their stakeholders that they are still on course towards their objectives. If this is the case, they should take the opportunity to invest spare resource and capacity in developments that will help them survive less tranquil waters. Managers and staff often have undeveloped ideas for projects and innovations, just waiting for the time to explore and implement them. Now is that time. For example, a common sustainability challenge is about how to manage growth – how do organisations scale up a successful delivery model or transfer it to a new area, without taking their eyes off the ball and putting existing activity at risk? This should be less of a conundrum when there is spare capacity in the team. Spare budget could be used to recruit staff (to develop the new area or provide cover for existing services), commission a feasibility study, or run a pilot.

People should be encouraged to recognise this as an important opportunity to build capacity for the future, and to get on with developing the new products, services or approaches they have dreamt of. More mundanely, it might be that the organisation can invest in new stock and equipment, again provisioning it for future opportunities and challenges.

Stakeholder strategy: Involve

If cruisers are *not* on course towards their objectives it makes sense to involve stakeholders in checking and redirecting them. Similarly, if things are going well for good reason, this is an ideal opportunity to involve stakeholders in conversations about the future. Time and resources should be available for consultations, evaluations, stakeholder engagement events, service reviews, planning meetings, away days – things that are always useful but are usually less pressing than operational demands.

It is likely that when things are going well, stakeholders and sustainability will be overlooked. But now is exactly the right time to excite people around a vision for the next stage in the organisation's development. If organisations wait until things are on a downward curve before they promote their vision and enlist support, they become a much less attractive prospect for people to invest their time, money and effort in. It is much more attractive for supporters to invest in a positive vision for the future than to fill a hole.

Section summary – the Paradoxes, Principles and Practices of sustainability

Paradox/ Myth	Principles	Practices
The Change Paradox	Sustainability ≠ sustained	Adapt and evolve purposefully. Encourage experimentation. Prioritise and embed learning. Reflect, learn and share intelligence.
The Octopus Paradox	Diversifying activity ≠ reducing risk	Focus on the core – core purpose and core structure. Stop the funding merry-go-round. Provide strong leadership. Develop income generation strategies and idea screening matrices. Align and engage with policy.
The Yes/No Paradox	Sustainability > money	Assess organisational and sector sustainability. Manage capacity. Understand when, how and what to say 'no' to.
The Efficiency Paradox	Sustainability ≠ efficiency	Balance scrutiny and strategy. Review costs. Invest in capacity. Welcome deviation. Allow for slack. Facilitate collaboration and attend to negative effects of competition.
The myth of perpetual motion	Sustainability ≠ self-sustaining	Build capacity to make a lasting difference (i.e. sustainability). Share understanding of sustainability.

Table 2: The paradoxes, principles and practices of sustainability

These paradoxes, principles and practices lead us to five capabilities organisations need to develop to sustain their work or its impact:

- Involvement
- Income generation
- Innovation
- Improvement
- Impact measurement

Part Three explores these in detail.

PART 3: THE FIVE CAPABILITIES

If we follow each of the sustainability paradoxes and principles to their logical conclusion, we can identify a number of additional practices that help to sustain organisations and their impact. These are the skills and abilities organisations need to develop in order to survive – and make a lasting difference. They are the five capabilities of sustainable organisations. They are highly interconnected so should not be thought of as a logical, linear sequence, but we will explore them in this order:

- Involvement
- Income generation
- Innovation
- Improvement
- Impact measurement

Each capability is made up of two elements. These will be used to structure the chapters that follow. For each element, I present six key indicators and ideas for action that can be used to assess and develop an organisation's sustainability capabilities.

Capability	Elements
Involvement	Participation – Discovering what people want and need.
	Partnership – Working together for a shared purpose.
Income generation	Pounds and pence – Holistic understanding of where revenue comes from.
	Profile – Internal and external engagement with and from key stakeholders.
Innovation	People – Investing in development.
	Pioneering – Active learning and experimentation to find new solutions.
Improvement	Purpose – Unity and clarity of vision.
	Planning – Systematic but responsive processes.
Impact measurement	Proving – Evaluating effectiveness.
	Policy – Using evidence to influence and inform.

Table 3: An overview of the five capabilities and their core elements.

Each chapter begins with a series of *provocations* to encourage a fresh approach to the capability being introduced. The elements are made up of six simple indicators. Although these describe what an organisation can do to develop the Sustainability Capabilities, they also leave room for interpretation. Unlike the practices suggested above for reconciling the paradoxes, there are no easy or 'right' answers as to how an organisation should proceed. Indeed, I encourage you to think critically about each indicator and how it can be applied to your organisation. They have been developed, tested and used by every imaginable size and type of organisation in every part of the non-profit world, from multi-million-pound international organisations to volunteer-led community groups. But each has found its own answers and approaches to the indicators. After all, if there were a simple formula to follow to guarantee sustainability, it wouldn't present the existential challenges it does.

Appendix 1 collates 60 indicators into an easy-to-use self-assessment grid. This is also available as a writeable PDF as part of the Lasting Difference Toolkit. It can be downloaded free of charge from www.TheLastingDifference.com.

CHAPTER 10: INVOLVEMENT

Provocation: Who does your organisation's work belong to?
Where is the power and where does it need to be?
How do you ensure that people's voices are heard without being tokenistic?
When carrying out consultations, how many voices need to be heard?
How can technology be used to increase involvement?
Do the most intelligent people all work for your organisation?
Do organisations have relationships? Or do people?
How does your organisation assess potential partners?
How do you feel about working with partners?

Involvement is the glue that holds the other Sustainability Capabilities together. Fundamentally, your work will only survive if it matters enough to other people that they will willingly support and stand up for it. And you can only make a lasting difference if you work in ways that recognise people's innate motivations, skills and aspirations.

Non-profit organisations might be expected to be more committed to (and reliant upon) involvement than their commercial counterparts. But there has been a shift in values in recent years, with organisations in every sector recognising that people and communities:

- Do not want to be passive recipients of communications, services or support. They want to be involved in creating the experience they receive.
- Want relationships not transactions.
- Are a tremendous source of ideas and innovation. They can help organisations make sense of an unpredictable, complex world, consciously or through their behaviour.
- Are more loyal when they are more involved. Loyalty builds support. Support builds sustainability.

From...	**To...**
Passive	Active
Consumers	Creators
Recipients of services and messages	Participants in shaping services, ideas and content
Fickle value seekers	Loyal value creators
Transactions	Relationships

Table 4: A shift in values in how organisations and communities interact

If you're not convinced, think about the last time you did one of these things:

- *Used a loyalty card*
- *Read, wrote or forwarded a social media post*
- *Read or posted an online review*
- *Gave your email address in exchange for free resources*
- *Took part in an online poll or survey*
- *Gave a donation or organised sponsorship*
- *Signed a petition or took part in a campaign.*

Each of these activities reflects the shift in values described above. Of course, some of the involvement tactics used by different companies are more altruistic or ethically motivated than others. But in the non-profit world, sustainability will arise from people feeling a genuine sense of 'ownership' for, and connection with, your organisation. Are they familiar with your organisation or services? Do they identify with it and see their interests and values reflected in it? Do they have a say in how it is designed and delivered?

This is partly about managing the Change Paradox, by making sure your organisation's work is founded on up to date evidence of aspiration and need. And it's partly about answering the question: if your organisation were no longer around, who would feel its loss? These are the people who should have a stake in its survival. This will equip different organisations with different resources that can be used to support sustainability:

- Having the legitimacy that comes from *representing* people (in large numbers or by virtue of a specialist understanding).
- Being able to mobilise support, e.g. participation in fundraising or campaigning, particularly if the organisation's survival is threatened. Support also takes the form of people's willingness to contribute ideas and suggestions, e.g. to consultations, evaluations and reviews.
- Efficient and effective promotion using word of mouth support from advocates. Messages from 'the horse's mouth' are particularly valuable because they are independent and based on real-life experience.
- Addressing power imbalances – the people who would feel a non-profit organisation's loss are likely to have less power and authority than the people who might be more able to influence the organisation's survival.
- Working with partners, who are more likely to be successful if you are successful – and vice versa.

THE ELEMENTS OF INVOLVEMENT

The Involvement capability is made up of two elements: *Participation* (finding out what people want and need) and *Partnership* (working together for a shared purpose). Each of these is explored below, using six suggested indicators that can be used to develop ideas for action.

Involvement 1: Participation

Participation 1: Be clear on who you want to reach with your work.
To be sustainable, organisations need to define how much 'reach' is enough. There will always be more work to do, so at what point will staff, trustees and other stakeholders be satisfied with the type and amount of work the organisation does? It is important for organisations to be clear about their target audiences and focus their work and resources on them. Who are they? Where are they? How many of them are there? What characteristics do they have, e.g. demographics, behaviours, resources?

From a funder's perspective it is vital that non-profit organisations can provide recent and accurate evidence of the *need* for the work they are proposing, based on the genuine involvement of people who will benefit from it. This has become increasingly important in recent years and, in the UK, it is a trend that will continue as more emphasis is put on local planning and decision-making. Funders, commissioners, non-profit regulators and inspectors are all stepping up their expectations of community or service-user involvement in and ownership of decision-making.

Participation 2: Identify the needs and aspirations of your organisation's stakeholders and the people you work with - and change your services in response to these.
Needs and aspirations must be identified systematically and analytically. It's risky to base decisions on hunches about what people want from your organisation. The difference between *thinking* you know and actually *knowing* is important.

- Analyse past trends – who funded your organisation and why?
- Who used your services, and why?
- Why did they choose to come to you and not somewhere else?
- Ask people – what matters to them?
- How do they define the things they want from your organisation?

People within organisations are used to thinking of their organisation from the inside out. They take a 'supply side' view of things. But when they find out about their organisations from the outside in, a 'demand side' view, they begin to understand what people need from the organisation and, hopefully, why they value it. For example, if my local train company perceives itself only as a train company, it might complacently think it has no competition: there's only one station nearby and only one company that offers trains along it. But from my 'demand side' perspective, I need transport not a train. So, the train company is competing with other public transport providers like bus companies, as well as private transport like my car and bike. Getting this wrong, failing to see the company from the outside in, has caused the downfall of many firms. Even the process of finding out what people want can be a powerful way of signalling that you are interested in them and want to serve them well.

The second part of the indicator is of course about the Change Paradox. It's one thing to know what people want, it's another to be able to change your services, activities or ways of working based on it. But as we have seen, if your organisation doesn't do this, it will become unsustainable over time.

Participation 3: Understand the types and levels of involvement people want to have and provide a range of appropriate opportunities for them to do so.
Organisations often find that when they carry out a consultation, survey or focus group, it's always the same people who contribute. Different people will want different types of involvement and you need to make it easy for people to get involved, whatever their preferences. For example, some people might be happy to speak one-to-one, others in groups. Some might prefer written communication, others more visual, creative or participatory. Does your organisation provide opportunities for people to give their views out of hours? As part of their everyday contact with you? In imaginative ways? With different technologies?

The same goes for *levels* of involvement. Again there will be different preferences, with some people wanting relatively little involvement (for example in consultation and decision-making) and others wanting to help steer the organisation (having a board is a form of volunteer involvement). Levels of involvement are usually represented as a spectrum. The International Association for Public Participation has really helpful resources based on a spectrum called IAP2. In Scotland, VOICE uses the simplest spectrum I have come across, from informing people to consulting and fully engaging them.

Figure 9: The VOICE spectrum of involvement (Scottish Community Development Centre)

It is worth stressing that these spectrums identify information-giving as the vital first step in involvement. People need to be able to contribute informed views and make informed decisions, so they need good access and good information. Importantly, this also includes giving feedback to them on what has happened as a result of their participation.

Participation 4: Involve people in exploring different ways to run or sustain the organisation, service or impact.

This indicator is explicitly about being open to people's ideas about the future of your organisation or service. Remember the organisation's work will only be sustainable if it matters to people. Who are these people, and what are their views on how they would like things to work in future? What new ideas can they offer for running and sustaining things?

Organisations I work with are sometimes reticent about involving beneficiaries or other stakeholders (including staff) in explicit conversations about sustainability. They might not want to scare people, especially people who rely on their services. But who does the work belong to? Who would feel its loss if it wasn't there? Involve people early on in conversations about sustainability. This way it can be discussed and planned for when things are going well, without fear or pressure.

Participation 5: Be clear on the outcomes and benefits of involvement, for both the organisation and the people it works with.

Organisations often take a supply-sided view of involvement, knowing what they want to find out about or get from it. And if they are not exactly clear on why they are involving people, they shouldn't! Do you want to inform people about something? Do you want to consult with them? Do you want to engage and empower them to do something? What's in it for them? A basic principle is that people shouldn't be worse off by taking part – so for face-to-face events, provide transport costs and appropriate catering as a minimum. But involvement can offer much more than this. Sometimes prizes are offered as incentives, which is fine, but it's tacit acknowledgment that people don't actually want to take part. Wouldn't it be better if people wanted to help? I believe they do, but we need to find ways to allow this to be expressed.

For example, can you run activities that people want to be part of, and use some of the time or activities to find out the things you need to? Information sessions, engaging away days, free training, special meals (business breakfasts, networking dinners), free downloadable resources in return for answering a few simple questions, access to social media forums where people can get and contribute information. Can people learn valuable new skills by working alongside you to design a consultation or evaluation, conducting interviews and focus groups and helping to analyse information?

Sometimes the more you ask of people the more they will be willing to give. For example, I've found that people might not bother to read organisational newsletters (supply-sided pushing of information) but they will happily give up a few hours to come to a consultation event that gives them something in return (e.g. information, access to networks, or even just the opportunity to help something they care about).

Participation 6: Prioritise accessibility and equality. Other than your eligibility criteria there should be no barriers to full participation.

When it comes to involvement, some people are more visible and vocal than others; some are more empowered. If these are the only people who get involved in an organisation's work (for example in consultations and evaluations) this will perpetuate itself. Organisations must make extra effort to identify and remove barriers to participation. They can carry out or commission accessibility and equality audits, enlist the help of organisations with specialist knowledge of the groups they are trying to reach, and ask people with lived experience of particular barriers what they think would improve accessibility for other people like them. This is an example of reciprocity, one of the principles of involvement. To be sustainable, organisations must be open to not knowing all the answers, not being the experts, and allowing themselves to harness the goodwill of their supporters.

Involvement 2: Partnership

Partnership 1: Develop good, up to date knowledge of other organisations, their priorities and what can be achieved by working together.
Every organisation needs partners. They might be suppliers or contractors, organisations working in a similar field, or formal partners in alliances and joint ventures. The important thing is that once we realise this, we realise organisations within our networks are mutually reliant on each other's sustainability (see the illustration at the end of this section on why partnership is integral to sustainability).

This has a few implications. Firstly, organisations are more likely to do well if their partners around them are doing well. For example, if organisations in a particular sector (social care, environment, education etc.) successfully influence policy in their area of shared interest, they can all benefit. Conversely, if the same organisations are struggling financially, this will have an impact on their partners, who might have to put more resources (time, staff, effort) into a joint venture; there will also be a knock-on effect on suppliers (fewer contracts, delayed payments etc.).

Thought about in this way, your organisation is not in competition with other organisations. But your network might be in competition with other networks. So, it is important to understand the organisations around yours. Can your organisations achieve more or work more efficiently by working together? Can you attract funding by developing partnerships? Single-issue organisations might find it useful to collaborate to develop partnership responses to complex social problems, e.g. a charity for ex-service personnel might partner a homelessness charity to combat homelessness among veterans; a mental health organisation might partner an older people's organisation to research depression in elders; a micro-enterprise organisation might partner an equalities organisation to empower marginalised communities.

This indicator is also about understanding partners' agendas and priorities. It is not always possible to anticipate how partnerships will turn out, but organisations should enter into them with open eyes, alert to the risks and opportunities they bring. Lots of research exists about the indicators of effective partnerships – shared goals, agendas and values are obvious things to look for. It is also likely that staff and managers know instinctively when a potential partner organisation is a good fit. Learning about these partnerships and how they develop is a valuable way to add new insights into the 'idea screening matrix' mentioned within the Sustainability Paradoxes above.

Partnership 2: Do things with your people and partners, not to them.
'Nothing about us without us' is a core principle of Involvement. As with all principles it looks simple and easy to follow but requires more in application. For example, who decides when to involve people? Who decides what to involve them in? Who makes final decisions about strategy, direction and how resources will be used in pursuit of it? Every organisation will struggle with these dynamics of power and representation, even member-led cooperatives and mutual aid organisations.
Organisations need to acknowledge these challenges and compromises but not let them stop them from trying to live up to the principle. As a guiding principle it remains core to non-profit sustainability. Doing things in partnership strengthens connections, redresses power imbalances and increases independence. Organisations' connection to the people and organisations around them is a form of protection.

Partnership 3: Staff, volunteers, participants and stakeholders are partners in your organisation's success. Involve them in the things you do and the decisions you make.
There's a lot in this indicator, so let's break it down.

- *Partners in success*

In the commercial worlds of law and accounting, there are few greater rewards than the status conferred by being a 'partner'. Partners have a say in the running of the organisation and because they contribute to its success, they benefit from the rewards. To what extent do people feel like partners in your organisation's work?

- *Having a say*

Each organisation will have limits on the extent to which it wants or allows people to have a say in its running. Again, this comes back to the spectrum of involvement. Does your organisation have a range of levels and ways in which people can contribute to decisions and direction?

- *Contributing to success*

Does involvement contribute to success? For example, is your organisation harnessing the ideas and innovations that happen every day - or crushing them? Can internal and external partners look at the organisation's work and say, 'I contributed to that'?

- *Rewards of success*

The rewards will almost certainly be different to those in the commercial world – sometimes in the non-profit sector the work is the reward. So how does your organisation ensure that people benefit from the success they contribute to? Are working conditions better? Do they receive a better service? Do they receive recognition? Is this done in a way that they value? External partners often want their branding to be used in partnership work, for example funders' logos are normally required on publications and donors will often want – or be pleased to have – public acknowledgement. After running a fundraising event, a care home in my area makes a point of telling donors not how much money was raised, but what it will be used for. Donors reportedly take more pride in knowing, for example, how many leisure activities were funded by their donation, than in knowing how much money was raised.

Partnership 4: Encourage partners and communities to share ownership of your organisation's work, e.g. identifying which parts of projects they could support, make referrals to, fund or deliver.

As noted above, organisations should be explicit about why ownership matters for sustainability – their work will not continue unless it 'belongs' to the people it serves. Again, stakeholders want to know how they can help and what difference their help will make. Non-profit organisations don't always have a clear 'ask' of their supporters, or they feel diffident about being direct about it. So, how clear is your organisation about what it needs? If it's money, how much, what for and when do you need it by? If it's knowledge, what kind, how will it be used? If it's time, what difference will it make and what will people get in return? Once organisations are clear on this, it is easier to identify who can help and how to go about asking them.

Partnership 5: Link your organisation's systems and ways of working with other organisations', where appropriate.

This indicator is about understanding how other organisations' processes and timescales work and making things easy and efficient by aligning with them where possible.

For example, if you know that a funder needs a report in October it makes sense to gather data and begin writing a few months before. If a hospital refers people to your service in the month before discharging them, should you process referrals monthly or weekly? If you and a partner both gather information when assessing people or places, can you reduce duplication (and burden on people) by combining your paperwork? This is a tangible example of the Paradoxes of Efficiency and Change – if we are not adaptable to the world around us, we will not be as efficient or relevant as we must to be sustainable.

See the additional chapter at the end of this section for more illustrations of why partnership is integral to sustainability (Chapter 11 below).

Partnership 6: Ensure your partners understand how effective your organisation is. Collaboration helps your organisation to harness resources and achieve things it couldn't do alone.

It is important to note the wording of this indicator – it's not that you *think* people *would* describe you as effective, it's that they *do*. When did you last ask partners what they think about your organisation's work? Do you hold partnership review meetings to reflect on progress at regular intervals or upon reaching certain milestones?

The second part of the indicator is a reminder that collaboration should be purposeful and that all parties should always be clear about the mutual aims and benefits of working together. Partnerships need constant maintenance to make sure they are effective and beneficial to all. Involvement is an investment and needs to be resourced. It also needs persistence, patience, respect, trust and reciprocity.

Involvement: Summary

Participation

- Be clear on who you want to reach with your work.
- Identify the needs and aspirations of your organisation's stakeholders and the people you work with - and change your services in response to these.
- Understand the types and levels of involvement people want to have and provide a range of appropriate opportunities for them to do so.
- Involve people in exploring different ways to run or sustain the organisation, service or impact.
- Be clear on the outcomes and benefits of involvement, for both the organisation and the people it works with.
- Prioritise accessibility and equality. Other than your eligibility criteria there should be no barriers to full participation.

Partnership

- Develop good, up to date knowledge of other organisations, their priorities and what can be achieved by working together.
- Do things with your people and partners, not to them.
- Staff, volunteers, participants and stakeholders are partners in your organisation's success. Involve them in the things you do and the decisions you make.
- Encourage partners and communities to share ownership of your organisation's work.
- Link your organisation's systems and ways of working with other organisations', where appropriate.
- Ensure your partners understand how effective your organisation is. Collaboration helps your organisation to harness resources and achieve things it couldn't do alone.

[The indicators above are presented as a self-assessment tool in the Appendix.]

CHAPTER 11: ILLUSTRATION

Why partnership is integral to sustainability

Organisations (and, in biology, organisms) are traditionally depicted as a series of inputs, activities and outputs, as in Figure 10.

They take in resources from their external environments (inputs) and transform these through their processes and activities into outputs – the product of the transformation. For example, a sawmill's inputs include things to be transformed like timber, and things that enable the transformation like staff, machinery and electricity.

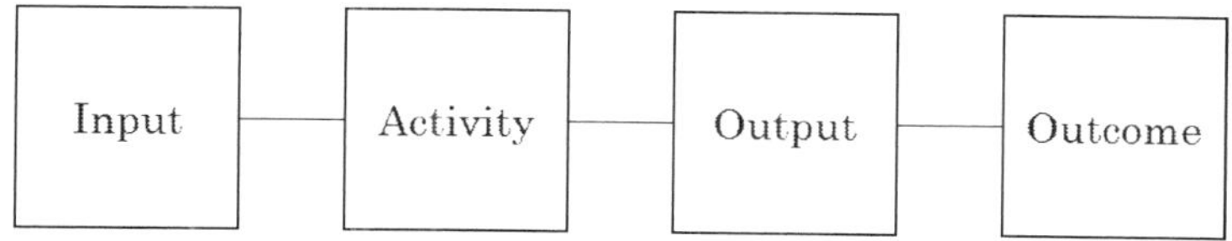

Figure 10: A transformation model. Note the addition of outcomes in the non-profit sector.

Over time, companies have moved the focus of their customer interaction from right to left. Once, they were purely interested in selling their outputs and customers were targeted as relatively passive recipients of marketing communications. Then organisations began to realise they could make savings and perhaps add value to the customer experience by involving customers in the 'activity' stage. Using the customer as labour might sound risky, but it is the business model behind the success of firms like IKEA, where customers pick their own orders from the warehouse, arrange their own delivery and assemble their own products. Self-service in cafes, airport check-ins and supermarkets is another form of this approach, sometimes called 'shadow work'. In the non-profit world, voluntary labour may be used simply to deliver services or as a route to enablement and empowerment. For example, some social care organisations promote self-management to enable people with long-term health conditions to live fuller, more independent lives.

Marketing strategies are no longer just about selling outputs. They seek inputs and involvement.

More recently, customers have even begun creating their own inputs. For instance, the most popular websites and social media channels are based entirely on user-generated content. News agencies invite the public to share photos and reports (traditionally reserved for qualified journalists and accredited photographers) and even opinions (traditionally the preserve of editorial staff). Corporate marketing strategies are no longer just about selling outputs. They are seeking inputs.

In the non-profit organisation things are less straightforward. The inputs to be transformed tend to be more complex – they are often human (people, communities) or intangible (knowledge, ideas).

Commercial organisations might sell the dream of the outcome that follows consumption of the output (a car maker might advertise the freedom or prestige that we will experience when driving their car). But unlike non-profit organisations, no-one actually expects the dream to be achieved – or measured. The transformation model stops at the production of an output. Non-profit organisations on the other hand are fundamentally interested in the end outcome – making a difference (and measuring it).

The basic transformation model doesn't show the interconnectedness of organisations. A linear relationship is implied – see Figure 11. Supply chains provide an organisation's inputs; once they are transformed, the company's outputs become inputs for other organisations and networks such as sales and distribution companies. The number and interconnectedness of stakeholders, and the addition of outcomes, makes this much more complex for non-profit organisations.

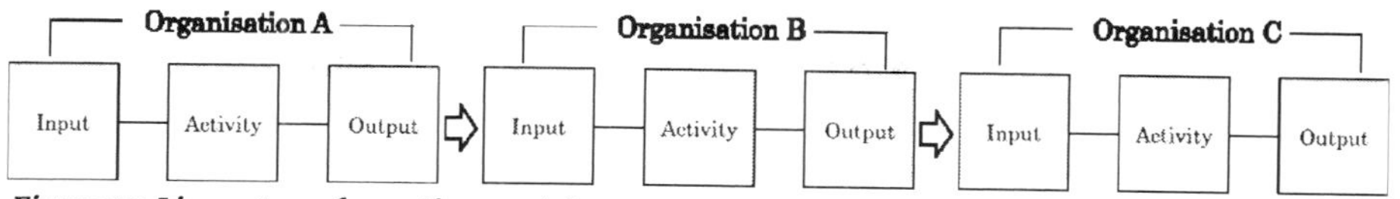

Figure 11: Linear transformation models

There are many ways in which a non-profit organisation's transformation model links with other organisations, but some of the most important in terms of sustainability are described below using two organisations, Organisation A, (shown in grey) and Organisation B (shown in white).

Organisation A's outputs, Organisation B's inputs

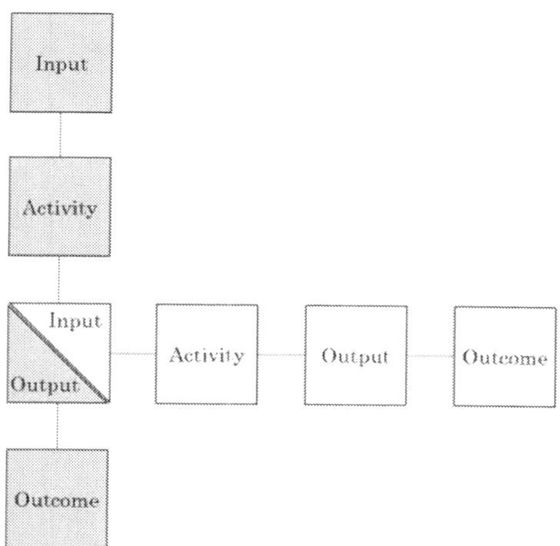

Figure 12: Two organisations' transformation models and how they interlink

As with the example mentioned above, a non-profit organisation's inputs usually come from another organisation's outputs. For example, outputs from suppliers like manufacturers, wholesalers, designers and printers provide resources for non-profit organisations to use. Relationships with these suppliers are therefore important for ensuring quality and cost-effectiveness but can be overlooked, as non-profit organisations can be more focused on the process or outcome of transformation.

Another aspect of the output/input relationship that can be overlooked is that one of the main inputs for non-profit organisations is knowledge. For example, Organisation A might provide intelligence about developments in Organisation B's field. It might carry out research (activity), producing evidence (output) that Organisation B can use in its own work. If we think about it in this way, organisations need good relationships with and access to providers of knowledge and information. Non-profit organisations often provide this function for each other, perhaps as members of learning networks or communities of practice. But as we saw with the Octopus Paradox and the Efficiency Paradox, time and space need to be created to take part in these relationships and exchanges.

Organisation A's outcomes, Organisation B's inputs

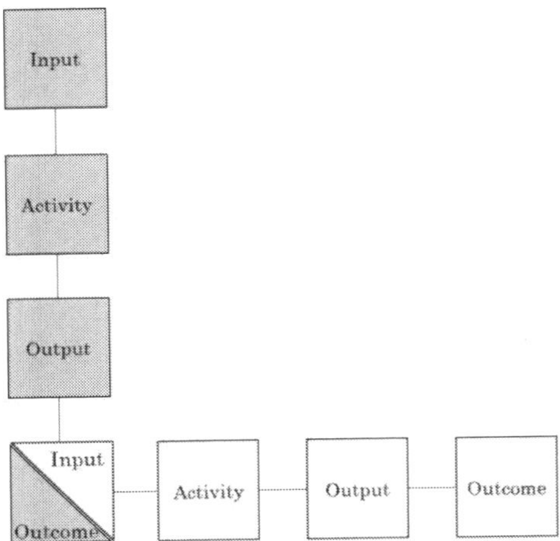

Figure 13: One organisation's outcomes become another's inputs

Non-profit organisations exist to make a difference (outcomes). In this instance, Organisation A's outcomes provide Organisation B's inputs. For example, if Organisation A is a college, one of its main outcomes is more highly educated students, which become an input (qualified staff) for Organisation B. Similarly, if Organisation A is a rehabilitation centre, its outcomes might be people who are ready to live independently. If Organisation B is a housing provider, it needs these inputs to achieve its own outcomes (which might include reduced homelessness, ability to manage a tenancy and so on).

Of course, outcomes don't have to relate to people, they might be about environments. For example, if Organisation A's outcome is to increase the availability of green space around a city, this provides a valuable resource for Organisation B to use for its own outcomes, increased outdoor activity. In the example below, it is also possible for organisations' outcomes to overlap.

Organisation A's outcomes, Organisation B's outcomes

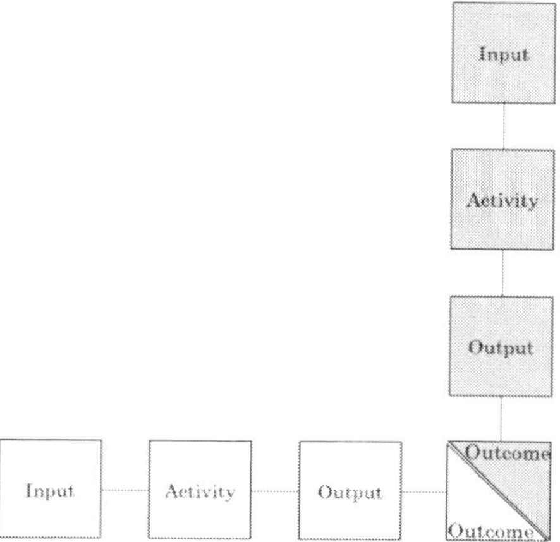

Figure 14: Organisations with shared outcomes

In this scenario, Organisation A and B's work overlaps by having the same or similar outcomes. It would be hoped that this would be the purpose of any partnership or collaboration, ideally with each partner achieving something that they could not have achieved alone. For example, if Organisation A is a youth work charity and Organisation B is a smoking cessation organisation, together they might achieve the outcome of reducing young people's smoking.

Of course, Organisation A and Organisation B might both be required to report to their funders and boards about the difference they have made, and the vexed question of attribution arises – whose outcome is it? When the end result has been achieved, does it matter who claims it? When funding and stakeholder support hinge on being able to evidence outcomes and impact, it matters a great deal!

This challenge can blight any partnership, so partners (and their stakeholders) need to recognise the distinctness of each other's contributions - and the collective impact they share. Thankfully, evaluation fashion is moving on from 'attribution' (knowing who or which intervention made the difference) towards 'contribution' (knowing that a difference was made, and how interventions contributed to it). And funding fashion is placing renewed emphasis on partnership approaches. However, attribution is always likely to be an element of partnership work, so outcomes need to be identified and agreed as clearly as possible. In the example above, perhaps Organisation A's distinct outcome could be increasing young people's access to information about smoking. Organisation B's could be increasing their knowledge and ability to make informed choices. The combined outcome would still be the same and should still be celebrated.

Organisation A's inputs, Organisation B's inputs

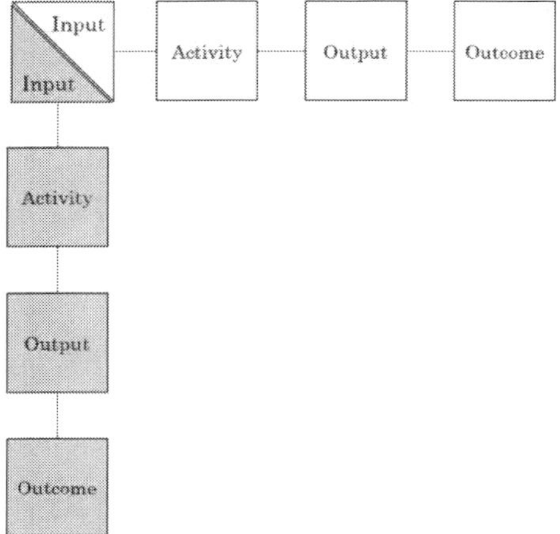

Figure 15: Two organisations with shared inputs.

When two or more organisations share the same inputs, there is potential for competition, particularly if those resources are finite. Competition for funding and stakeholder support means that non-profit organisations have become adept at preparing compelling evidence and funding applications. Larger organisations have teams dedicated to fundraising, tendering and business development. These teams are sometimes so efficient in pursuit of their goal (maximising income for their organisation) that they become ruthlessly competitive. In the UK in the last few years, there has been national outcry about charities hounding donors for money. But this hasn't stopped sharp practices when it comes to tendering for public contracts or applying for grant funding. The public is losing its faith and trust in charities as a result.

There is of course an alternative. Having to access limited resources can lead to effective collaboration.

Case study: Self-direction and collaboration in the Scottish Highlands

In 2014 I carried out a review of a new approach to social care in the Highlands of Scotland (now mainstreamed in the UK as Self-Directed Support). Rather than the traditional model of the local authority holding a budget for individual care, individuals and families were given personal budgets to purchase and manage their own support. When I interviewed service providers, I expected them to tell me about the increased competition brought about by the requirement to access the same level of funding from a market that was now much more dispersed.

Indeed, service providers reported facing many challenges, not least having to market themselves to thousands of potential customers, not just one (the local authority). They also needed bigger, more flexible workforces, as individuals wanted to use their personal budget for more personalised services, which might include out-of-hours or specialist support. People also wanted local support, a significant challenge in a large and remote region. These challenges were so great and the resources (staffing, time, money) so limited that organisations realised they had to collaborate to survive.

If someone wanted support in a remote town where their chosen organisation had no staff or presence, the organisation had to be able to draft in staff from one of their partners. If someone wanted specialist support that their preferred provider was not able to offer, the provider needed to call on another organisation's expertise - and share the budget with them. To do these things, organisations needed good knowledge of each other's work, so they formed networks across the region, meeting regularly to discuss developments, plan services and share workloads. They also needed to be pragmatic – collaboration helped them access resources they didn't have. But, more importantly, it let them make a difference they could not have made alone.

Resource scarcity calls for imaginative responses, and non-profit organisations will need to continue developing these capabilities. The reflex response does not have to be the competitive one.

At the same time, partnership works best when it is entered into willingly – we can't force people to be our friends. Organisations A and B above might have had to work together on the smoking cessation project because a funder wouldn't back either project alone but would support a partnership. This sometimes happens when funders receive similar-looking applications from similar-looking organisations and encourage the organisations to form consortia and joint ventures. As in the example above, this can help leverage different organisations' resources and experience to impact different parts of people's lives. But realistically, this practice of requiring partnerships can also further increase competitive practices – unwilling partners are unlikely to want to share their ideas and learning or leave them unprotected.

The important thing to remember is that organisations do not operate in a vacuum. Their resources, activities, outputs and outcomes are all reliant on and interconnected with countless other organisations. This is harder to conceptualise, and navigate, than the simple transformation model above. But if organisations underestimate the importance of participation and partnership, of involving people in their work, they become closed systems and will wither like un-watered tomatoes in a greenhouse. They will not have the capacity to make a lasting difference.

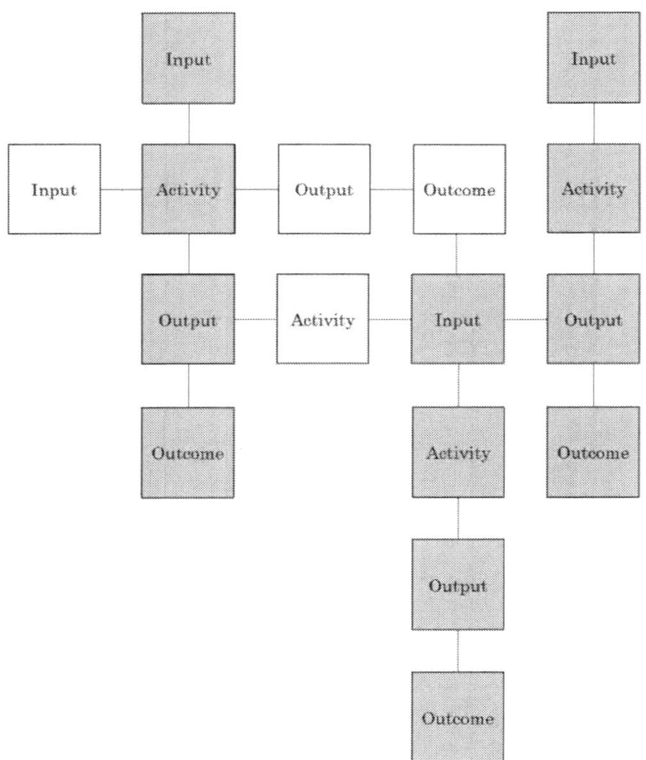

Figure 16: In real life, organisations are interdependent, with complex webs of inter-relationships with each other. They do not and cannot stand alone.

CHAPTER 12: INCOME GENERATION

Provocation: Money follows good work, not the other way around
Should your organisation try to earn more – or spend less?
Are the people who bring in your organisation's revenue (e.g. fundraisers, business development teams) connected to its everyday work? How well do they know the people who benefit from their efforts (e.g. internal colleagues, external beneficiaries)?
Are your sustainability challenges about funding – or communications, marketing or stakeholder engagement?
Are you prepared for what happens if your organisation's marketing strategy is successful?
How well known is your organisation? What does it want to be known for?
Are donors, funders and commissioners aware of what your organisation does – and what it can do for them?

Most people think about non-profit sustainability in the context of money. And it's a very big part of the picture. After all, if organisations didn't need money, sustainability wouldn't be so much of an issue. But it's not sustainable to carry on earning and spending and earning and spending without taking time to think:

- Where does your organisation's money come from?
- What is it trying to achieve with it?
- What has it done with money it already had? Was it used wisely? What difference did it make?
- What does it need more money for?
- What will it do when the money is gone again?

In other words, money is not enough to guarantee sustainability. There are many other things that can make an organisation unsustainable. If you think back on your own working life, you will almost certainly have worked for, or know of, an organisation that was financially healthy but otherwise unsustainable. Trustees were maybe unfit to be on the board; governance might have been questionable; management practices and decision-making might have been poor; staff might have been untrained, unsupported, undeveloped; clients and purpose may have taken second place to other things...like income generation.

Income generation is a necessary but insufficient approach to sustainability because money does not exist in isolation from any of the factors above. It comes from stakeholders (*Involvement*) who want to know good work is being done (*Innovation and Improvement*) and that their money makes a difference (*Impact Measurement*). Sustainable income generation, in other words, relies on the four other capabilities.

Sustainable income generation relies on the four other capabilities and cannot be achieved in isolation from them.

Successful income generation strategies are based on analysis and take a holistic approach to all of an organisation's sources of revenue. The elements and indicators below are designed to help you to carry out a holistic sustainability assessment.

Note: When I use the words 'income generation' I refer to all of the possible sources of revenue for a non-profit organisation, including:

- Donations (including legacies)
- Grants
- Contracts
- Trading
- Sponsorship (including corporate and crowd fundraising)
- Investments

In the past, some people used 'income generation' as a euphemism for trading, calling everything else 'fundraising'. For clarity, I deliberately talk about 'income generation' to encourage a broad and holistic view of all potential sources of revenue.

THE ELEMENTS OF INCOME GENERATION

Income Generation 1: Pounds and pence

Pounds and Pence 1: Develop an effective, holistic income generation strategy that aligns marketing, communication, stakeholder engagement and fundraising.
This indicator is about two main points. Firstly, non-profit organisations should have a clear strategy for income generation, ideally a written one (a free template is available from www.TheLastingDifference.com). This should ensure that all revenue-generating efforts are aligned with the organisation's purpose and strategic plan (and each other). It should help to resist the pull of the Octopus, giving managers and trustees clear parameters for the sorts of income – and income generating activity – that are needed.

The second point leads on from this. Some organisations operate like they have a big, empty funding pot, and the more money that can be thrown into it, the better. This means they often have quite different purposes for and messages about generating income. For example, large charities often have separate teams for grant fundraising, events and donations, business development and tendering, marketing and communications. It is unusual to find all these working towards the same strategy – other than filling the pot. Is that what you want your organisation to be known for? Smaller organisations can have the same problem, for example not recognising that their communications and stakeholder engagement are also valuable marketing opportunities.

That's why a holistic income generation strategy is required. It aligns revenue-generating functions with each other and with the overall organisational strategy. It helps organisations ensure their limited resources are pulling in the same direction. And, most importantly, it means stakeholders receive clear, consistent messages they can understand and support.

Pounds and Pence 2: Identify and review your organisation's true costs and make sure these are covered by funding. When this is not the case it must be for clearly expressed strategic reasons.

Financial sustainability requires income generation – keeping the bath taps running with new inputs. But it also requires plugging the drain - reviewing costs and outgoings. Organisations need to critically assess their ways of working – do all activities contribute to sustainability, or do they drain resources?

Costs need to be reviewed so that managers and trustees can make decisions based on accurate information about the true costs and effectiveness of activities and commitments. Yet it is surprising how often managers are unable to identify or evidence the true costs of their organisation's work. This is sometimes to do with the complexity (or perceived arbitrariness) of assigning indirect overhead costs to budgets for projects and services. But it is well worth doing. Not only will it give trustees the ability to make better-informed decisions, it will give funders reassurance that yours is a well-governed, cost-effective organisation.

The second part of this indicator is about making sure your organisation always has clear and strategic reasons for doing work that is not fully funded. I have been a member of and supported boards who have in effect decided to make significant subsidies to or investment in initiatives *without realising this is what they were doing.* Although this is scary to witness, it is not unusual. It is what happens when a board approves a deficit budget because not all of an organisation's sources of revenue or funding have yet been identified for the year ahead. They gamble (hopefully based on informed decisions based on previous trends) that the revenue will come throughout the year.

It is also what happens when an organisation accepts contracts or funding that don't cover the full costs of the work. Again, there is an implicit decision that this is an investment and that the reward is worth it. Organisations must look more closely at these 'investments' and be more critical about whether there is any return and whether it is worth it.

Is this a contract worth winning?
At what point do you think the commissioner will agree to increasing the contract to allow you to break even?
Why would they pay for something you are already giving them free?
How many customers of this kind can you carry before you bankrupt your organisation?

Now, these managers are not stupid or reckless. They know the rational sense in these questions. But they are under real pressure to maintain revenue, generate turnover, keep staff in jobs and maintain services for people in need. In these circumstances, any money can look like good money.

Boards and senior managers must be able to recognise these situations for what they are and make clearer strategic decisions about them. If they are investments, what's the expected return? What else could have been invested in with the same money, and what would that return be? Is the organisation using its limited revenue to fill holes - or to build something for the future?

Case study: recovering full costs

An organisation I worked with identified that they had been subsidising a contract from a public-sector commissioner for over 10 years. They had only ever calculated and charged for direct costs, not indirect costs or overheads. When the commissioner decided to put the contract out to tender, the charity had a dilemma – if they bid at their existing rate they would continue under-charging for the work. But if they used the accurate rate, the commissioner might think they were exploiting the opportunity to bump up costs. As it turned out, because the charity could, for the first time, explain that the bid was based on an accurate appraisal of costs, the commissioner understood. In another example, I was supporting a group of social care organisations in a sustainability-themed action learning set. Like the example above, two of them were in the process of re-tendering for existing services in different parts of the country. Each of them won their respective tender, only to find that the commissioner then wanted to negotiate the price downwards. And in each case, when the organisations showed the commissioners that the cost they quoted was based on sound calculations, the costs were agreed and the negotiation ceased.

Pounds and Pence 3: Ensure funding comes from an appropriate range of sources. To understand income generation in context, your organisation's income must be systematically analysed. A simple spreadsheet like the one below looks pedestrian but can be an incredibly powerful tool for understanding your organisation in news ways.

Source	Year 1	Year 2	Year 3	Year 4
Donations				
Grants				
Contracts				
Trading				
Sponsorship				
Investments				

Table 5: Example format for an income analysis spreadsheet

Once you have populated a spreadsheet like this, it is very easy to maintain, helping you to spot trends, identify key sectors and supporters, and make plans for retaining them – or finding new ones.

The table can be segmented to provide more detail and more interesting data to work with. For example, break 'donations' down into individual, family or corporate; or do they come from events or legacies? Or break 'contracts' into local or national; public, private or voluntary sector and so on. Other columns can be added to calculate the lifetime value of a supporter or sector; the number of supporters in each segment; the cost (or time) involved in acquiring or retaining a supporter; changes in value over time etc.

The important thing is to use the data dynamically – look for trends over a period of years and answer these questions in order to help plan for future income generation:

- How many sources of revenue does your organisation have?
- Do you know why customers and supporters chose to give their money to you?
- What value do you add for them in return?
- Do you know when and why any of them stopped giving?
- Is this the right funding mix or would you like it to change?
- Based on trends to date, how long will it take to achieve the desired blend?

Pounds and Pence 4: Be clear on the value your organisation can add to funders without being led by their requirements.
This indicator is about avoiding the Octopus by aligning funding with your organisation's own outcomes and purpose – not the other way around. Having clear criteria for assessing which types of revenue to pursue makes your income generation efforts more efficient. Increasing alignment improves your chances of success. Funders usually know when organisations' purposes are genuinely aligned to their own and when they are just being led by the funding.

As with the indicator above, it can be extremely valuable to find out why people chose to support you – so ask them! This indicates to them that you appreciate their support, but it also gives you valuable intelligence for attracting other similar supporters.

Pounds and Pence 5: Actively track when funding for projects or posts is due to end and put plans in place to review or renew it. Involve staff and trustees in this.
Although managers are likely to know and track when funding is due to end, the information is likely to be in their head, and the burden on their shoulders. The best fundraiser I ever worked with made visual representations of funding to help staff and trustees understand how people's posts and projects were made up; when each portion of funding was due to end; what she was doing about it – and what she needed from them. She used timelines to let people see into the future (trustees especially appreciate this).

Specific breakdowns of projects and job roles were also made, showing the different sources and levels of funding that contributed to them. This helped staff and trustees understand the complexity of the funding mix and the connections between different strands of activity and funding. It united everyone in the organisation in contributing to its future.

Pounds and Pence 6: Identify and take action on financially failing projects.
The term 'financially failing projects' is slightly harsh and might mean different things in different organisations. Typically, it would refer to a project that is neither covering its own direct costs or the contribution to overheads that has been assigned to it. Monitoring both of these factors is important. There may be strategic reasons to support a project that doesn't contribute its share of overheads. And we must recognise that even the best developed models for calculating full-cost recovery contain an element of arbitrariness. So, we should be cautious about making decisions using this measure alone. But a project that is not covering its own costs requires action. Costs may need to be cut, extra funding may be needed, or the project may need to be closed.

Again, this comes back to being able to make well-informed strategic decisions. If organisations arrive at a position of financial un-sustainability, which many will periodically do, it should not be because boards and management were sleepwalking into the problem. Understanding costs and revenue in a holistic way is a vital part of this process.

Income Generation 2: Profile

Profile 1: Your organisation's approach to raising its profile should be in line with the impact it wants to make for communities and stakeholders.
I have yet to meet a non-profit organisation that doesn't want more profile than it currently has. This aspiration doesn't just come from staff and trustees, but also from external stakeholders. We must be slightly cautious about this because non-profit organisations will always want to be able to reach more people, and for more people to be aware of their important work. Will enough ever really be enough? Nevertheless, the indicator is a useful touchstone. If your organisation's profile is lower than it needs to be to achieve its intended impact, does the profile need to increase – or do ambitions need to be lowered? Most non-profit organisations would be uncomfortable with the latter, so will probably want to do something about the former. Indeed, if your

organisation is diffident about publicising its work, this indicator might help to overcome this.

Profile 2: Identify your existing and potential markets.
Some people will find the word 'market' inappropriate in a non-profit context. But I find it a helpful metaphor because non-profits are involved in service and exchange - people give them things in return for something else. It helps to be clear on who these people are and what they want.

- Beneficiaries might give non-profits their time and trust. In return they will hope the organisation can make a difference to their lives or environments.

- Funders must also give their trust, not just because they are giving money they want to be managed properly, but because they invest their name and reputation in the organisations they support. Non-profit organisations must reciprocate by demonstrating good governance, effective operations and, usually, evidence of impact and learning.

- Policy and decision-makers also give their time and trust in return for convincing evidence of need – and solutions. Non-profit organisations have to 'sell' a particular message or discourse in a crowded marketplace.

- Staff, volunteers and trustees give their time, skill and effort in return for safe, satisfying opportunities to make a difference.

Examples like these are why it is so important to understand your organisation from a stakeholder or customer perspective.

In terms of identifying potential markets, this again requires analysis. Looking at your income analysis spreadsheet (see above), which stakeholders share the same characteristics as those who have already supported you? Who shares the same needs and aspirations?

Remember from the exploration of transformation models in Chapter 11 that your organisation is also in the market for inputs. The better your market of suppliers is, the better you will be able to serve your other markets. What are your potential markets for obtaining intelligence, insights, staff, volunteers and other valuable resources?

Profile 3: Promote your organisation and its projects with clear messages, to clearly identified audiences, using appropriate methods.
Imagine you are hosting a dinner party and plan on cooking for your guests. What's the first thing that comes to mind? You will want to know who is coming, what they like to eat, what you have available, and what you are capable of cooking well. You might want to anticipate dietary requirements. But it's a fair guess that crockery will be near the bottom of your list. When it comes to promoting your organisation, it makes sense to do things in the same order.

- Identify who you want to reach and serve and what they might want from you (the market).
- Work out what you can offer them and what you want to tell them (the message).
- Then, and only then, think about the best way to get the message to them (the medium).

Organisations often focus on the medium first. People who work in marketing or communications are all too used to being asked to produce a leaflet, website or campaign, without a clear brief about who it is for or what it needs to convey. No analysis has been done, no strategy has been developed. Ask for one and people will look at you blankly, like the manager in Chapter 5 who believed fundraising £1m was important for its own sake.

It's about being clear who your organisation wants to serve, what they need and how it will do it. In this regard, profile *is* strategy. Marketing or communications staff should be represented in senior management teams for this reason. In smaller organisations, it would make sense to have people with these skills on the board, or at the very least, keeping promotion and communications in mind when developing strategy. Market before messages before medium. Guests before food before crockery.

Profile 4: Measure the effectiveness and cost-effectiveness of the promotional and income generation work your organisation does.
As the old adage goes, 'Half the money I spent on advertising is wasted, the trouble is I don't know which half'. It is not easy to accurately measure or attribute success to promotions. However, useful metrics can still be developed to help focus limited time and resources.

- Where did people hear about your organisation?
- What percentage of funding applications and proposals are successful?
- Has the rate changed over time?
- Can it be affected by increased focus and targeting?

- How much is spent on different types of promotion and how many contacts do they generate? (This lets you calculate a cost of acquiring new clients or business. When combined with an average client/segment value (e.g. from the analysis spreadsheet above) this is helpful for working out whether investments are cost-effective).

A useful first step can be to assess your existing marketing and promotional materials and whether they are generating *awareness, interest, decisions* or *action* (known in the marketing world as AIDA). Traditional marketing approaches (leaflets, advertisements, websites etc) tend to raise *awareness* and, if they are effective, generate *interest.* But stakeholder *decisions* and *actions* tend to come from higher-bandwidth communication like meetings, events, presentations, conversations etc. This isn't to say that money and effort spent on generating awareness and interest is wasted. It's just that awareness and interest are only the foundation for decision and action. Assess your current promotional methods to make sure the focus is where it needs to be.

Profile 5: Ensure colleagues at all levels (e.g. managers, staff, trustees) are clear on their role in promoting the organisation.
For chief officers and senior managers, this goes back to the idea of the figurehead or hood ornament, understanding the promotional purpose of looking up, out and ahead of the organisation. For managers it's about being able to identify needs and trends, design services and negotiate contracts with funders and other partners. For staff it means understanding the importance of what marketeers call 'moments of truth'. These are the moments when real life customer service has the ability to live up to – or let down – the promises that advertising and promotion have made. If there is a gap between customer expectation and reality, there is a problem. If they are unexpectedly delighted, it's a nice problem, but it probably indicates that your organisation is underselling itself. And of course, if they're disappointed it indicates that the advertising was misleading – or the service was poor, both of which need to be addressed urgently.

In this way of understanding organisations, dedicated marketing functions are redundant to the extent that it's everyone's job to promote the organisation, with consistent messages. Although this sounds harsh, I've yet to meet a marketing person who disagrees. They can't carry the task of promoting the organisation alone, and they can't do it well if there's dissonance between strategy and execution, promises and reality.

If your organisation lives up to this indicator, the function of marketing staff becomes to coordinate the different types and levels of stakeholder engagement that take place. This includes advising and briefing chief officers, for example before a press interview or fundraising event. As well as coordinating effort, marketing staff can collate and interpret the intelligence that comes back and develop strategies in response. Again, even if you work in a small organisation there's a simple principle here: when it comes to promoting your organisation, remember the importance of listening. Effective marketing is about understanding and meeting people's needs.

Profile 6: Identify advocates (e.g. participants, partners, referrers) who can help to promote your organisation's work and reach new audiences.
Even large organisations have finite resources for raising their profile. And messages are more convincing and powerful when they come from an independent source. So, it pays to identify who your advocates and supporters are. This might mean asking permission to use positive feedback on websites and brochures. It might mean asking people to forward social media posts, introduce you to their networks (in person, via an app liked LinkedIn or simply referring a friend). Or it could be a more public endorsement like speaking at a conference, telling their story to somebody new to the service, or being filmed talking about your work.
Again, non-profit organisations can sometimes be hesitant or diffident about asking for this support. The challenge is less likely to be identifying people who are vocal supporters of your work, it might be more about having the confidence to ask them. Part of this is allowing yourself to ask for help. It is important to remember that reciprocity is an important principle of involvement. You might be surprised not just at how willing people are to tell their story, but how grateful they are for the chance to do so.

Finally, non-profit organisations are increasingly turning to joint approaches to marketing and promotions. For example, they may form networks to raise awareness of issues they have a mutual interest in promoting, come together to form consortia for funding bids, or agree to promote complementary messages.

Income Generation: Summary

Pounds and pence

- Develop an effective, holistic income generation strategy that aligns marketing, communication, stakeholder engagement and fundraising.
- Identify and review your organisation's true costs and make sure these are covered by funding. When this is not the case it must be for clearly expressed strategic reasons.
- Ensure funding comes from an appropriate range of sources.
- Be clear on the value your organisation can add to funders without being led by their requirements.
- Actively track when funding for projects or posts is due to end and put plans in place to review or renew it. Involve staff and trustees in this.
- Identify and take action on financially failing projects.

Profile

- Your organisation's approach to raising its profile should be in line with the impact it wants to make for communities and stakeholders.
- Identify your existing and potential markets.
- Promote your organisation and its projects with clear messages, to clearly identified audiences, using appropriate methods.
- Measure the effectiveness and cost-effectiveness of the promotional and income generation work your organisation does.
- Ensure colleagues at all levels (e.g. managers, staff, trustees) are clear on their role in promoting the organisation.
- Identify advocates (e.g. participants, partners, referrers) who can help to promote your organisation's work and reach new audiences.

[The indicators above are presented as a self-assessment tool in the Appendix.]

CHAPTER 13: INNOVATION

Provocation: We are all creative, but we need time, trust and permission to play. And, at times, to fail.
How are new ideas greeted in your organisation?
Would your organisation rather sustain services – or impact?
What different delivery models and organisational structures have been explored?
How does involvement contribute to innovation?
Do staff feel they need to wait for permission to try new things?
Whose permission do you need to do the right thing?

Sustainability does not mean sustained. The Change Paradox tells us that organisations need to keep adapting, changing and evolving in order to survive. This means being prepared to find, develop and test new ideas. Crucially, it means organisations being able to let go of the ideas and behaviours which got them to their current point, but which will hold them back in future. We cannot do this without innovation. Innovation is the process of exploring, identifying, selecting and testing ideas.

Sadly, one of the very ideas that holds this back is that innovation is something other people do - 'creative' people. The idea of the creative genius is deeply entrenched in our world view. And it's a romantic idea, the thought that sparkling new breakthroughs come from the ether, to the muse-inspired genius. There are problems with this myth.

Firstly, innovation is hard work. It requires patience, not just accepting the first idea that comes along. I still regret hearing a bootlegged demo of The Beatles in my youth – they weren't geniuses, they were...rubbish! How was that possible? What I didn't appreciate was that 'creative geniuses' draft and redraft their ideas, looking for other, better ways to express things, ways of refining and improving the original idea. Iterating through stages of drafting, design and development is a key component of innovation. That's because there is a qualitative and purposeful aspect to innovation – novelty is not enough.

Play, prototyping and testing also matter, to make sure time is not wasted on the wrong ideas. This can be hard for perfectionists, who tend not to get things completed because, of course, things will never be perfect. In fact, it's very useful to be able to identify in the different people around you those who:

- Are good at generating ideas
- Can develop them
- Can critique and refine them
- Can market and sell them.

Innovation is a process with distinct stages, and nobody will excel at all of them. Knowing this simple fact, and helping others understand it, can make team work a lot less frustrating.

Early in the innovation process, it is important to go wide, encouraging divergent thinking to generate as many ideas as possible. The people in your team who are quick thinkers, visionary, perhaps a bit leftfield (you're not always sure what they're talking about or why it matters to them) are needed at this time. Importantly, you shouldn't assume this stage is about finding ideas to solve a problem. It can be more effective to spend time exploring and reframing a problem first, to make sure you are addressing the right one. At this stage the perpetual critic who says *'Ah, but...'* and *'The problem with that is'* can be very unwelcome. They can kill creativity before it even starts. So, signal to people that there will come a time for them to use those skills (and they are skills), but it's not now.

Conversely, once ideas have been developed and you need to narrow down a range of options, the left-field 'creative' thinker can kill creativity. Still coming up with new ideas, or perhaps protective of their original vision, they can stifle the appraisal and critiquing stage, finding it hard to accept a solution when there are so many more ideas to explore. At this stage, the more methodical, critical, analytical thinkers excel. They can weigh up options coolly, spotting flaws not because they are 'negative' people but because this is their way of helping to improve innovations.

The myth of creative genius is inaccurate because we're all creative. Now, I'm one of those people who cringe when people tell me that anyone can draw, sing, or play an instrument - I really can't. But I do believe we are all creative. Because creativity isn't reserved for the arts alone. In your workplace the people who believe they are the least creative are often the most innovative. Finance clerks design spreadsheets that do things non-financial people never thought were possible. Administrators make improvements to their processes every day of the week. Policy officers excel at finding imaginative ways to interpret and present arguments. Support workers help people make simple adjustments in their lifestyles that are transformational. Environmentalists create habitats so that life emerges where there was none before. People innovate every day of the week. If the only innovations were those that came from creative geniuses, there would be very few indeed.

Innovation does not mean making dramatic new discoveries and breakthroughs. Although that can happen, it is very rare. Real innovation is much more about incremental improvements in (or repurposing of) things that already exist. As Carl Sagan the cosmologist said, 'If you wish to make an apple pie from scratch, you must first invent the universe'.

THE ELEMENTS OF INNOVATION

Innovation 1: People

People 1: Make sure the organisation's vision, culture and ethos are clear and attractive enough for people to commit themselves to.
High-quality innovation comes from people freely contributing their efforts and ideas because they believe in them and the goals they are contributing to. Organisations cannot mandate commitment or innovation, but they can and must remove the things that inhibit them.

Your organisation's vision and ethos need be clear enough for people to remember and embody in their everyday work. In smaller or newer organisations this will help create an overall culture of innovation. People will have the confidence and clarity to make decisions without having to ask or await permission. In larger or older organisations, it's not enough to express the desire for innovation in a strategy document, everyday practice has to embody it.

People 2: Encourage the development of innovation, ideas and inspiration.
Provide support and encouragement for innovation and ideas to flourish. Examples include using team away days, training people in creative thinking and sharing learning. As noted above, people might not believe they can be creative, or have confidence in their ideas. Creating space (e.g. in away days) signals the organisation's commitment to people and their ideas. It provides opportunities for ideas to flourish away from the everyday pressures that can stifle them. Training people in, or helping them learn about, creative thinking and creative problem solving validates the view that they are already creative and that they have the abilities to contribute to organisational innovation.

People 3: Allocate time and resources to allow everyone to contribute ideas for innovation and improvement.
This partly echoes the indicator above about creating space, but it's also about investing time and resource. This will look different in different organisations. For example, two of my clients allocate half a day a week for staff to pursue their own development, typically allowing them to catch up on reading that never gets done otherwise. Other organisations will invest resource in new developments. This might mean assigning a budget to test a new model of delivery (for example designing and

testing a new training course). Or it could mean creating space and capacity by allowing the team or worker not to do one of their regular tasks while they explore a new development.

The other aspect of this indicator is about everyone having the ability and opportunity to contribute to innovation. Remember, the people who feel the least creative are often the ones who have the most valuable insights. Administrators, cleaners and security guards all observe the ways an organisation works. Contractors and clients experience this first hand. As with Involvement, time and resources should be invested to create opportunities for everyone in and around an organisation to contribute.

People 4: Encourage collaborative and networking activities which support problem solving, idea generation and celebrating success.
The best people don't all work for you. As noted in the book's introduction, organisations need porous boundaries that let people and ideas through in both directions. Again, this could take any number of forms: releasing staff to join communities of practice and working groups; contributing to online fora; forming consortia and joint ventures; providing internships and secondments; attending training and conferences and so on.

With limited time and resources, organisations need to be selective about the right opportunities to pursue. But it is a mistake to think that cutting training budgets, proscribing participation in partnerships or keeping an organisation's ideas to itself will do anything other than harm organisational sustainability. Find ways to keep innovation prominent by giving it regular attention, recognition and celebration. This must be done in ways that are comfortable for people and in-keeping with the organisation's ethos

People 5: Support staff and volunteers to develop within and beyond their current roles.
The best managers support their teams to perform their current roles well and to develop for the future. I believe people are motivated by learning. Once we have stopped learning in a role, and once we have contributed the main ideas and improvements we can make, it is time to move on. So, counter-intuitive though it may seem, people contribute more innovation and ideas when they see their current role as an opportunity to develop. To stay innovative and energised in a role, people benefit from being supported but they also want to be stretched. Once again, the form this takes can vary and may include job shadowing, mentoring, attending conferences, taking on additional responsibilities and so on. It is important to remember that if organisations stifle development they stifle innovation and, in turn, sustainability.

People 6: Leaders should act as change agents, challenging team members to critically explore and frame problems and encouraging innovative solutions.
Note that leaders of innovation might not be managers. In the iterative process of innovation outlined above it is likely that different people will take the lead at different times. The important thing is that leaders facilitate the process of innovation, but they can't and shouldn't try to control it. One of the most important things anyone in a team can do is remember the ideas of divergence (going wide) and convergence (narrowing in) and signal to the group which stage it is in, and what kinds of contributions are needed.

Exploring and framing challenges from different perspectives and in different ways is a vital stage in problem solving and design processes. It ensures the right problems are addressed, provides options to choose from, and unlocks creativity by allowing things to be seen in new ways. There are many tools and techniques for this. While they don't tend to change the fundamental nature of the challenge, they often change the way people can go about tackling it. To support innovation, leaders can create safe, supportive space for:

- Questions to be asked
- Debates to be aired
- Situations to be explored
- Problems and opportunities to be reframed from different perspectives
- Opinions and solutions to be held lightly
- Keeping explorations open until closure is required.

Innovation 2: Pioneering

Pioneering 1: Ensure your organisational culture encourages and supports innovation. Value experimentation, risk and failure within safe limits.

Innovation, experimentation, risk and failure are mutually dependent. If people and organisations don't try new things, they never develop. If things always go exactly as planned, they never learn.

I had not originally wanted to include the words *'within safe limits'* in the indicator, because I want to reinforce the point that experimentation and risk shouldn't just be tolerated (though they must be), they should be valued. They should be celebrated, even when things 'go wrong' – when something is an experiment, there is no 'failure' if you have learned something in the process.

However, the 'safe limits' caveat is important. Non-profit organisations have limited resources. Their main asset is often their reputation. Unless the sustainability challenges they face require a 'bet the company' level of gamble, organisations need to identify the parameters of their tolerance and appetite for risk.

- What do you want to test?
- What do you want to learn?
- How will you know you've been successful?
- And how can you protect beneficiaries, staff, the organisation and its partners if the experiment doesn't work?

If organisational culture can't be changed or if it inhibits motivation, some companies create separate teams or departments where unconventional wisdom can be pursued and organisational norms can be defied. For example, during World War II, Lockheed famously created what became trademarked as a 'Skunk Works' to research and develop aircraft, protected from the constraints of the organisation's processes and hierarchy.

Pioneering 2: Actively support organisational and service development. Capture the learning and exploit the opportunities that emerge.

In non-profit organisations pilots and projects are often developed in response to emerging needs and opportunities. But the extent to which they have an explicit role in generating learning within organisational culture (or, as illustrated above) away from organisational structure, varies. In the future, a learning emphasis will become crucial for sustainability. It is what most funders pay for, more or less explicitly (they either use funding as a form of informal action research to generate intelligence about a particular field of work, or they want to support organisations to learn and develop). And it contributes to sustainability by building organisational capacity, increasing understanding and providing new development opportunities.

The word 'exploit' might be uncomfortable for some. It arises from the observation that most organisations (non-profit or otherwise) under-use the resources they develop. This is perhaps a natural consequence of the 'do, do, do' cycle, but is inefficient and ineffective. Time and expense have been put into developing an asset (physical or intellectual), so it only makes sense that the asset should work as hard for the organisation as possible. For example, if your organisation researches and produces a policy briefing you would surely want it to be as widely read as possible. You might incorporate its messages into other publications, workshops and conference presentations. Similarly, if a project identifies an unmet need and is effective at addressing it, you would want to share that learning across the organisation, and perhaps scale the project up so that more people benefit. Yet it is common to observe organisations and managers putting more work into developing the next resource than making the most of the last one.

Pioneering 3: Work with other organisations to innovate new approaches to common challenges.
This indicator is about acting on the collaborative opportunities mentioned in the *People* element above. It is about using partnerships to share inputs, activities or outputs in pursuit of common outcomes. As with *Partnership*, this requires that we know our partners and potential partners well and have clear rationales for selecting and working with them. Common examples of this indicator in practice are:

- Forming consortia to fund joint work on a shared issue.
- Organisations in the same sector pooling resources to campaign, influence policy or raise public awareness.
- Partnership projects or job roles created to work across and share learning between two or more organisations.
- Universities working with other non-profit organisations to develop research.

Pioneering 4: Ensure information and innovations are shared effectively between staff, management and trustees.
Like profile, communication is something that every organisation wants to improve. In this instance, it is about ensuring that learning takes place across the organisation. This helps to spread good practice and avoid costly mistakes. It is also about having good links and communication channels so that everyone in the organisation is working towards the same goal and understands each other's role in achieving it.

Pioneering 5: Ensure problem solving and decision-making processes are inclusive and robust.

The 'inclusive' aspect of this indicator is mostly covered within the Involvement capability above. 'Robust processes' means that there need to be clear criteria for exploring challenges and making decisions.

- How many different alternatives are discussed and explored before a course of action is decided?
- What sorts of evidence does your organisation use, in what circumstances and in what ways?
- Is evidence used to inform opinions or to justify them?
- To what extent do research and experience inform and improve decision-making?

These questions will have different answers on different occasions and at different levels in the organisation. Agreeing the decision-making process before trying to make decisions isn't usually easy, but it pays off in the longer term because discussions will be more focused and decisions will be better understood and supported.

Pioneering 6: Become a learning organisation, using everyone's knowledge and skills to produce solutions to challenges.

Again, people within or around an organisation will have unique insight and can help it to innovate and develop. Knowledge needs to be created and shared. Organisations need to be explicit about the intent behind this to make sure learning is resourced, supported and used effectively.

Non-profit organisations' main assets are intangible and relate to knowledge and relationships. Creating and sharing knowledge is one of the most effective ways of increasing capacity to make a lasting difference (i.e. sustainability). To be sustainable, non-profit organisations need to develop the capabilities to innovate and use this learning to improve. This is the theme of the next capability: *Improvement.*

Innovation: Summary

People

- Make sure the organisation's vision, culture and ethos are clear and attractive enough for people to commit themselves to.
- Encourage the development of innovation, ideas and inspiration.
- Allocate time and resources to allow everyone to contribute ideas for innovation and improvement.
- Encourage collaborative and networking activities which support problem solving, idea generation and celebrating success.
- Support staff and volunteers to develop within and beyond their current roles.
- Leaders should act as change agents, challenging team members to critically explore and frame problems and encouraging innovative solutions.

Pioneering

- Ensure your organisational culture encourages and supports innovation. Value experimentation, risk and failure within safe limits.
- Actively support organisational and service development. Capture the learning and exploit the opportunities that emerge.
- Work with other organisations to innovate new approaches to common challenges.
- Ensure information and innovations are shared effectively between staff, management and trustees.
- Ensure problem solving and decision-making processes are inclusive and robust.
- Become a learning organisation, using everyone's knowledge and skills to produce solutions to challenges.

[The indicators above are presented as a self-assessment in the Appendix.]

CHAPTER 14: IMPROVEMENT

Provocation: How good is good enough?
Do you have the right balance between development and delivery?
When did you last review your ways of working?
How do you stop and not just keep doing more of the same?
How realistic is it to continue with just the structures and systems you have?
Can demand be managed?
When you are baking a cake, what happens if you keep opening the oven door to monitor its growth?

Improvement is about getting better all the time. This might be incremental, with gradual improvement taking place over a period of time. This approach has gained recent prominence in the form of the theory of 'Marginal Gains'. Developed by Team Sky cycling, it is rooted in the observation that when competitions are decided by small margins (fractions of a second in the case of track cycling), small gains in performance can accumulate into big advantages.

However, there comes a point where marginal improvements are no longer possible, or it is impossible to find new ways to change the existing formula. A new paradigm is needed. So, improvement sometimes also needs to be radical, with major improvements happening quickly. Like *Innovation*, bigger, more radical breakthroughs are less common but they do happen.

Whether improvements are marginal or radical, Improvement and Innovation go together, so the same organisational cultures and behaviours that support one should support the other. However, this is not always the case – in pursuit of improvement, many organisations have adopted quality assurance methodologies that require so much adherence to process that innovation gets stifled.

The elements of *Improvement* below are based on clarity and unity of *Purpose*, and systematic but responsive *Planning.* These not only help sustainable organisations to manage the Octopus and Change Paradoxes, they leave room for *Innovation* and contribute to continuous *Improvement.*

THE ELEMENTS OF IMPROVEMENT

Improvement 1: Purpose

Purpose 1: Ensure the organisation and its projects are united by a shared vision and identity that everyone understands.
People want to know that their work matters. At the time of writing, purpose is apparently the radical new management trend, with leaders learning to become more authentic. These are, of course, nothing new to the non-profit world where they have always been at the core of the way organisations and their leaders operate. But it still

pays to make sure your organisational purpose us clear and memorable. As has been noted, it's easy for people to lose sight of the bigger purpose, particularly when faced with sustainability challenges.

It's also common for the staff who work in projects or locations away from the organisation's head office to associate more with their own project or location than with the organisation. Beneficiaries might also affiliate themselves more with a centre or service than with the host organisation. This isn't necessarily problematic in itself. But it can lead to conflict when the organisation's purpose and priorities appear at odds with the service's – or vice versa. It can increase duplication (e.g. when different services use different systems, branding or paperwork), inequity (e.g. when different services use different pay scales), and confusion and dilution of impact (e.g. when internal and external stakeholders are not aware of the wider organisational context in which work takes place).

Unity should not be pursued for its own sake or because diversity is unhealthy - quite the opposite. But unity of vision is one of the key determinants of strategic success. Everybody needs to understand the role they play in sustaining the organisation and/or its impact.

Purpose 2: Values should be embodied in everyday practice. There should be ongoing reflection and learning at all levels of the organisation.
The reason for linking these two clauses in one indicator is that values are very valuable touchstones for organisational learning and decision-making. They can be embedded in everything an organisation does, including staff induction, training, support and supervision, appraisal and performance management. Each of these provides opportunities to support learning and reflection by inviting discussion about the extent to which staff have lived up to stated values – and experienced them being reciprocated.

Reflection on and learning about values can also take place in team meetings, strategic planning, evaluations and internal and external reporting. If your organisation aspires to become a learning organisation, embracing values in this way is usually a comfortable and manageable way to do it. It may be necessary to review and develop the existing values, however. If they are not being used in the ways described, they may merely be empty statements on a strategic plan and could ring hollow. To work well, they should be accurate reflections of the most fundamental, unchanging aspects of the organisation. The organisation's 'way'.

Purpose 3: Support and encourage teamwork, participation, empowerment, creative problem solving and idea generation.
This is an ambitious indicator.

- What would it take for these things to be in place in your organisation?
- What would it look like when people are creatively engaged around and energised by a clear purpose?
- How fully empowered are people to make decisions and solve problems?

Organisations have begun developing new organisational structures to support the sorts of culture and behaviour that use *Involvement* to accelerate *Innovation* and *Improvement*. This can include relatively low-key approaches like assigning people to teams that compete to generate new ideas and solutions; or exploring 'lean' methodology, an approach to efficient production which comes from 1980s Japanese car manufacture via 2000s Silicon Valley. In more radical organisations, work becomes structured around flexible project teams which coalesce and disperse around specific briefs and developments. People join when their skills and interests can be put to the service of the group and move onto other teams when no longer needed, or when new developments take over. The analogy that sometimes gets used for this is of a film crew, which is made up of many different trades and skills coming together to complete a particular project before dispersing onto the next one.

At the root of all of these approaches, and this indicator, is the belief that people and teams generate solutions when they have the space and opportunity to do so.

Purpose 4: Define success on the basis of the development of your organisation's people and the people it serves.
Improvement is about getting better all the time. And organisations can't get better unless their people get better and serve other people better. This could mean helping staff to develop capabilities within their roles (see *Innovation* above) or helping them cope with pressure and increase their capacity (see below).

In terms of developing the people your organisation serves, this is about defining success in terms of the lasting difference your organisation's work makes. Even if your organisation doesn't have direct beneficiaries as such, there will be people for whom you want to improve things. You might want to make politicians or policy makers better informed, make things better for your members or improve the environment for the population as a whole. So, while development is necessary for *Improvement* inside the organisation, success should also be measured by how well your work contributes to improving things for others.

Purpose 5: Navigate and manage external pressures to work within capacity without compromising your values.
This might seem obvious, but every organisation needs periodical reminders to uphold its values. External pressures (e.g. from funders, communities, competitors, the wider economy) can be so great that internal priorities sometimes take second place. Equally, organisations must revisit and use their values to manage capacity. For example, there's no point in having a strategy that states an intention to be high quality and person-centred if staff are so stretched that they have to fit people into standard services regardless of personal preferences.

A simple test of how well an organisation lives up to this indicator is to look at the objectives and values in its strategic plan and compare them with its expenditure (in the UK, the latter must be publicly available, and the former is likely to be). Whatever the strategic plan says, an organisation's real-life priorities and values are reflected in the way it uses its resources, particularly its budgets.

If there is dissonance between values as they are stated and enacted, it is possible that the strategy might have been developed with the specific intention of bridging the gap between rhetoric and reality. But there is equally a risk that it is because the board or senior management team lack reflexivity and self-awareness. Ironically, the dissonance will almost certainly be obvious to internal and stakeholders, who will not be able to unite behind the strategy, whatever its stated values are.

Purpose 6: Recognise when capacity is overstretched and take action to balance capacity and demand so that quality, safety and staff wellbeing are not compromised.
As noted elsewhere, it is possible for people and organisations to work beyond capacity, and I believe a great many of them do. It is important to recognise the signs as early as possible to avoid staff burn-out and the mistakes and compromises that are an inevitable consequence of having too much work to do in too little time. Once it has been recognised, there are two options for managing this situation - increase capacity or manage demand. There are different, but limited, strategies for each of these, some more palatable than others for non-profit organisations.

Pricing: It is possibly distasteful to non-profits to use pricing to manage demand, but I have seen the following approaches working in some organisations in some circumstances:

- Offering free services to all but charging people who are prepared to pay for quicker access.
- Asking for financial contributions to the cost of activities.

- Bringing groups together to pool individual budgets to purchase more substantial support than they could afford alone.
- Developing systems for mutual aid or in-kind contributions (for instance through Local Exchange Trading Schemes).

Service model development: Many organisations have developed technological responses to manage capacity and demand. For example:

- Some charity shops have moved online.
- High-volume low-value training can be offered online, saving costs and reaching more people.
- Advice can be offered using webchat services, saving staff time and travel costs.
- Text messaging can be used to check in with clients, with the option of follow-up visits where needed.

Other examples of service model innovation include providing information and support online or in groups rather than face-to-face or one-to-one; closing building-based services to provide more tailored services; and campaigning via online petitions and social media rather than marches and rallies.

Booking and queueing: Some organisations are able to manage capacity by scheduling work, for example by managing bookings and by queueing jobs or enquiries in different ways. These typically rely on an effective triage system to assess and prioritise enquiries. The triage function might be carried out by staff who deal with straightforward enquiries and filter those that go to more expert staff. Other organisations might assign more qualified staff to the triage. Perhaps counterintuitively, this can reduce demand on expert time by picking up high-priority cases earlier.

Adjusting staffing levels: It can be expensive and challenging, but many organisations might find no alternative than to adjust staffing to meet demand. For example, agency and sessional staff can be used where budgets and HR policies allow. In the long-term, it is often unavoidable that non-profit organisations develop like concertinas, expanding or shrinking staffing in response to fluctuating demand – and income. Both phases (growth and decline) can be hard to manage and can have a disruptive impact on morale and wellbeing.

Whatever options are taken, managing capacity and demand is a perpetual juggling act requiring both careful planning and responsive adaptation. These are explored below.

Improvement 2: Planning

Planning 1: Work to achieve and sustain results that meet or exceed the needs and expectations of your customers, staff and stakeholders.
To bring about improvement, plans need to be ambitious. Goals should be challenging enough to make the organisation stretch to achieve them. This provides impetus for change by focusing attention on the gap between the organisation as it now is and the organisation as it needs to be.

Learning from *Involvement*, plans need to be based on a clear understanding of what different stakeholders want or expect. And, looking ahead to *Impact Measurement*, results must be measured to ensure needs have been met.

Planning 2: Systematically measure and improve quality.
Independent quality assurance frameworks can provide a systematic way to measure quality and track improvements over time. Relevant examples for the non-profit sectors include EFQM, Trusted Charity (formerly PQASSO), Investing in Volunteers and Investors in People. However, as noted, frameworks that use adherence to *process* as a proxy for *effectiveness* have limitations in settings where:

- Complexity in the environment requires continual adaptation
- Innovation is required, including process innovation
- Effectiveness is to be measured in terms of impact, not fidelity to process.

In these situations (very common for non-profit organisations) sector-specific frameworks might be more valuable, or internal measures of quality need to be developed. Some organisations will already be required to adhere to other formal standards (for example, for regulation, accreditation, membership of professional bodies), so additional quality measurement may not be required.

It is important to select the right framework. It should be a good match for what your organisation is trying to achieve and for the time and resources it can afford to put in.

Planning 3: Strike the balance between planning and responsiveness. Strategic and operational plans should set parameters but leave room for creativity and emergence.
For most organisations, the opportunity to balance planning and responsiveness comes when they develop a new strategic plan. This should set clear parameters for what the organisation will do (and by definition, what it *will not*). But it should also allow for adaptation within those parameters. Chief officers need to be held to account for the strategy's success, but they also need to be afforded flexibility about how those goals are achieved. As Henry Mintzberg observed, strategy walks on two feet - one planned, the other emergent.

Some chief officers are opposed to strategic plans because they perceive them as a straitjacket. They might feel their trustees are trying to constrain them, or that they are being asked to predict the future, identifying what will be achieved (and they will be held accountable for) in three to five years' time. Mature conversations are needed about this, so the right balance can be found. This indicator provides a useful starting point:

- Why does planning matter, and to whom?
- Why does responsiveness matter, and to whom?
- What are the parameters within which creativity and change are possible?
- How will they be reviewed?
- Will the strategic plan itself be reviewed? How? And how frequently?

Planning 4: Ensure boards and/or committees are diverse, well established, and have the right skills and experience to guide your work. Review their make-up and effectiveness regularly.
The ideas in this indicator are gaining prominence in boards everywhere, with particular emphasis on achieving gender equality. However, board discussions on diversity can be tricky for many reasons.

- Boards may be used to recruiting by invitation and recommendation rather than by open recruitment. They may fail to see how this limits diversity.
- Trustees won't always have had the same sector experience or training as staff and may therefore have different understanding of equality and diversity.

- In some organisations, board selection is only open to people (or organisations) who are members of the organisation, or users of its services. This may be a necessary criteria, but is it sufficient?
- Discussing board diversity and make-up can seem like a criticism of the existing board rather than a legitimate governance issue.

In situations like these, it can be useful to ask:

- To what extent current board diversity and make-up reflects that of the organisation's current and future constituents (beneficiaries, communities, stakeholders etc.)
- To what extent trustee recruitment complies with the organisation's other recruitment policies.
- Whether a skills (and/or diversity) audit would help to identify any gaps in the board's make up (templates are readily available).
- Whether external facilitation of these discussions would help.

The goal is to arrive at a point where boards routinely review their make-up and effectiveness. Reviewing effectiveness can be done in different ways, whether formal or informal:

- Constituting a board sub-committee or short-life working group.
- Having a closed, board-only session during each meeting.
- Chairs having one-to-one meetings with trustees, perhaps annually, to allow individual and collective effectiveness to be discussed.
- Measuring performance against any Terms of Reference that exist for the board, for example during the focus of a board away day or an externally-facilitated review.

Planning 5: Take a holistic approach to risk management and identify and respond to opportunities and threats effectively.

Identifying risks and ensuring measures are in place to mitigate and manage them are key requirements of non-profit organisations and their boards. Risk assessments may be operational or strategic and are likely to include the identification of each risk, an assessment of its likelihood and impact, and plans for mitigating or eliminating the risk. These approaches, quite rightly, help to prevent risk to the organisation or its people by helping to avoid threats. But they are not holistic. If we are interested in sustainability, it is also necessary to be clear about the risks of missing opportunities.

This is something that will need more active attention, because operational demands will always be more pressing that developmental ones.

Opportunities are most commonly identified during SWOT or PEST/LE analysis as part of a strategic planning process. However, what usually follows is a list, not an analysis. As a result, nothing is done about the factors that are identified. Instead, potential opportunities should be assessed:

- How desirable are they?
- How likely or viable are they?
- What investment is needed?
- What can be done right now to find out?

Holistic strategic risk assessments should identify the risk of opportunities not being developed. Plans for mitigating this should be set out, making clear the organisation's strategic intent to pursue sustainability through *Innovation* and *Improvement.*

Planning 6: Continue to assess and refine your organisation's approaches, including services, staffing and structures.

If the right balance is found between planning and responsiveness, plans will be reviewed as time goes on. At a strategic level this requires a willingness to review the organisation's overall goals, making sure they remain relevant.

Organisational structures and staffing also need to be reviewed periodically. This typically happens in response to changes in funding. But it is also a crucial stage of strategy-making, ensuring the organisation has the knowledge and capabilities to implement its strategies successfully.

Operationally, it means being prepared to review and adjust ways of working to make sure they are always improving. But fundamentally, it means *learning to learn*. The indicators within *Improvement* are about continually planning, reviewing, adjusting and improving. Sustainable organisations take this to the next level by planning how they plan, reviewing how they review and improving how they improve.

Improvement: Summary

Purpose

- Ensure the organisation and its projects are united by a shared vision and identity that everyone understands.
- Values should be embodied in everyday practice. There should be ongoing reflection and learning at all levels of the organisation.
- Support and encourage teamwork, participation, empowerment, creative problem solving and idea generation.
- Define success on the basis of the development of your organisation's people and the people it serves.
- Navigate and manage external pressures to work within capacity without compromising your values.
- Recognise when capacity is overstretched and take action to balance capacity and demand so that quality, safety and staff wellbeing are not compromised.

Planning

- Work to achieve and sustain results that meet or exceed the needs and expectations of your customers, staff and stakeholders.
- Systematically measure and improve quality.
- Strike the balance between planning and responsiveness. Strategic and operational plans should set parameters but leave room for creativity and emergence.
- Ensure boards and/or committees are diverse, well established, and have the right skills and experience to guide your work. Review their make-up and effectiveness regularly.
- Take a holistic approach to risk management and identify and respond to opportunities and threats effectively.
- Continue to assess and refine your organisation's approaches, including services, staffing and structures.

[The indicators above are presented as a self-assessment tool in the Appendix.]

CHAPTER 15: IMPACT MEASUREMENT

Provocation: What could you achieve if you let go of the need to claim attribution?
What evidence is there that your organisation's models are effective?
Whose interests are served by evaluation?
Is evaluation incorporated into everyday activities?
What does good data look like for you, your funders and your people?
How well does your data provide both depth or breadth?
What data do you already have and how much more do you really need?
How will you use and share the results?
How can you help funders hear people's stories?

The words 'impact measurement' have different uses. For some people, impact just means the difference that has been made as a direct result of an intervention. For others, impact will be the longer-term result that the intervention only contributes to. For our purposes, I will use the term simply to describe making a difference and measuring it, at whatever level this takes place.

Impact measurement usually has two purposes, each of which is vital for sustainability:

- Proving: Being able to evidence the need for and effectiveness of an organisation's work.
- Improving: Learning about what works and changing things as a result.

Once the need for a piece of work is clearly understood, activities and resources can be focused on where they can be most effective. There will be baselines to measure progress against. Evaluation isn't left until the end; it's built into everyday practice. Projects have clear outcomes to work towards and systems are in place to measure them - and any unexpected outcomes that emerge.

As the work develops, everyone can learn about what's working and what's not – the people you serve, your colleagues, managers and boards, and your funders, donors and commissioners. Sharing this learning demonstrates that your organisation is committed to *Improvement.* It also builds trust, showing that it is competent and effective. Being able to contribute credible evidence will in turn help to influence organisational, local or national policy.

The problem with measuring impact therefore isn't about *why* it matters. It isn't even about *how* to do it: there are lots of tools and frameworks available to make it easy. It just takes time to think about how to make them work in your setting. The elements and indicators in this section should help you to do this.

THE ELEMENTS OF IMPACT MEASUREMENT

Impact measurement 1: Proving

Proving 1: Gather recent, relevant evidence of need, based on research and/or genuine consultation with a range of stakeholders.
Evidence of need supports sustainability because it ensures your work is relevant and focused. You might think you know what the situation or problem is that you are trying to address, but would other people agree with you, particularly those who are most affected by it? Once the situation has been accurately established, how much clarity and agreement is there on how it should be addressed?
So, as well as ensuring the right activities are focused in the right areas, this indicator also encourages stakeholder support. And, pragmatically, it will increase your chances of convincing funders to support you. As the demands on their resources grow, funders need convincing evidence of accurately-assessed need and appropriately-designed interventions.

Proving 2: Use good quality evidence from a range of sources.
Organisations have a tendency to over-rely on one or two sources and types of evidence. Beneficiary feedback may be the main way of measuring impact in some organisations, while in others this may be dismissed as soft, anecdotal or biased evidence. In reality, every source and type of evidence has its flaws. The key to manageable and convincing evidence is to use information from a range of sources, something evaluators call triangulation. The term comes from cartography, where objects in the landscape need to be viewed from different perspectives to represent them accurately on a map. In the same way, evidence of impact should come from and be tested from a range of perspectives: beneficiaries; third parties (e.g. referrers, partner organisations, family members); staff (e.g. via observations or client records). Organisational records and artefacts (e.g. attendance records, products of activity) are often overlooked but provide easily available ways of verifying other evidence.

Similarly, a balance between qualitative and quantitative information ensures that a rounded picture is presented in evaluations. Each of the two types of data has its advocates – and its detractors. But they are best thought of as complementary parts of an overall whole, not as either/or alternatives to each other. Each helps to identify questions that the other can answer.

Quantitative data, typically gathered in surveys, questionnaires, registration forms etc. provides breadth, helping to understand *what* is happening, *where* and in *how many* cases. For instance, if an organisation provides keep-fit classes, quantitative information can show how many people signed up, how many dropped out, which activities and times of day are most popular and so on.

Qualitative data, typically gathered through interviews, focus groups or individual case notes and action plans, provides depth, helping to understand *how* and *why* things are happening. Without this, the keep-fit organisation won't know why people choose to continue – or drop out, or why some classes are more popular than others. Qualitative and quantitative information go together like yin and yang, each embodying different values, but working together to form a coherent whole.

Proving 3: Systematically evaluate your organisation's work and outcomes.
The emphasis on systematic measurement is shared with the *Improvement* capability above. But in this case, the system must be specific to your organisation. This is because outcomes (typically defined as the *difference* that comes out of your work) will also be specific to your organisation. At the very least, they will look or manifest differently to how they would anywhere else. For example, several organisations could share the desired outcome of *improving the health* of people in a particular community. But they would achieve and measure this differently. One service might promote healthy eating and measure changes in diet, while another might provide opportunities for exercise and measure people's activity levels.

A simple evaluation framework can help to make evaluation systematic, proportionate (and not burdensome) for staff or beneficiaries. For projects or small organisations, it needn't be any more complicated that identifying a small number of outcomes to be achieved (typically between three and six is about right), a range of indicators (measures of success, based on what the outcome would look like in practice – see examples above), and the methods that can be used to capture or record information.

If your organisation uses evaluation tools developed by another organisation, check that the tools really will evidence the outcomes and indicators you have selected. The important principle here is that when it comes to measuring outcomes, one size does not fit all, however rigorous and well tested it appears to be.

Proving 4: Evaluation should help your organisation to learn and improve. Use it to find out what works – and what doesn't.

Doing evaluation for its own sake, or purely because a funder requires it, is pointless. It's also unethical, collecting information that isn't going to inform anyone or change anything. Sadly, these things happen, often because the balance between proving and improving is wrong: organisations or services might think evaluation is about justifying their existence and nothing else.

So, it's vital for organisations to be purposeful about their approach to evaluation and make it their own. When organisations realise evaluation is about learning and improvement, they can redress power imbalances and make evaluation work for everyone:

- Beneficiaries and stakeholders get the chance to reflect on progress and plan their next steps (vital for empowering people and increasing independence).
- Staff get satisfaction from knowing they make a difference (not just thinking it), and how to improve their impact.
- Managers learn about which interventions are more effective than others.
- Boards, funders and other strategic stakeholders learn about what sorts of initiatives to invest in in the future.

The other benefit of keeping learning at the heart of evaluation is that if an evaluation tool or process is not helping you to learn anything new you can stop using it. Too many organisations gather feedback they don't really need, putting extra burden on their beneficiaries and staff. Again, having a systematic evaluation plan will help you to work out not just what you need to collect but when. Evaluation can and should be done as part of your everyday work, but that's very different from saying you need to evaluate everything all the time.

Proving 5: Evaluation should inform future planning. Review your work before developing new services or projects.

This takes us back to the 'Do-Do-Do' cycle. Even when organisations plan their evaluations systematically and gather data effectively, they often don't have (or take) time to use the results to inform their next steps. This means they are not using evaluation to improve, with the result that they can end up repeating mistakes, continuing ineffective work or drifting off-course.

It's also useful to remember that one of the first questions a new funder will ask is *'How do you know there's a need for this work?'*. They will also ask how it will be evaluated. Make your job easier, and theirs, by showing how last year's evaluation has informed this year's funding application or project design. For example, you might use your evidence to show that you were successful in reaching one target group, but not another. Maybe this new project has been designed to help you learn about this new group's needs and how best to serve them.

Although it can sometimes seem like funders are more interested in evaluation for proving than improving, this is not usually the case. If organisations use evaluation and reporting only to justify their existence, they probably won't exist very much longer.

Proving 6: Communicate evaluation findings with key stakeholders (participants, partner organisations, funders etc.).

Sustainable organisations know that evaluation and PR (public relations) are two different things. Good evidence can inform promotion and publicity, but that's not the reason for doing it. As part of a sustainable, knowledge-based ecosystem, organisations should use their evaluation results to help other people learn about what works and what doesn't. Some managers are averse to this, thinking that 'negative' results will harm them. They should ask themselves what is more convincing, a report that describes everything going perfectly, or one that also reflects on what could be improved. Organisations that only report success show themselves as lacking in self-awareness and reflexivity – or as dishonest. Even if a project were somehow wholly successful in every respect, reports should ask questions about how things could be improved and sustained – or how more stretching targets could be set – in future.

The other important principle in this indicator is that of reciprocity. If stakeholders are involved in an evaluation (for example, they give feedback, take part in surveys, show up at focus groups) they should be involved in the results. Organisations that wonder why no-one wants to take part in their evaluations have probably forgotten this.

Impact measurement 2: Policy

Policy 1: Identify the local and national strategies your organisation's work contributes to and make reference to these in your own strategies.
It might seem strange that *Policy* is part of the *Impact Measurement* capability. But the *Policy* element and indicators matter because the longer-term, higher-level contribution of your work cannot be measured easily or attributed to your work alone. Being able to link your activity and outcomes to other strategies helps you to show your contribution more clearly and credibly. It also lets you draw on any evidence and research that has already been done, helping to inform, and to some extent, make the case for, the work you are doing.

The sustainability risk here arises when strategic planners and commissioners don't know your organisation or work contributes to theirs (see Policy 4 below). For instance, operational staff within public sector services might value the work your organisation does for the clients that they refer. But if their boss's boss doesn't know this, why would they commission or fund the work?

Policy 2: Scan the external and policy environment to identify developments in your field.
This is about staying alert to important trends and changes that take place in the world around you. Even if an organisation does everything else in its power to be sustainable, it could still be at the mercy of the policy and funding environments in which it operates. Organisations need good awareness of developments so that they can anticipate and react to them, even if they can't influence them.

This is another reason *Partnership* is such an important element of sustainability – intelligence about developments on the horizon often comes from partners, networks and communities of practice.

It is also a reason why organisations should retain or develop some policy capabilities. It may not be possible for your organisation to reach policy makers, much less influence them. But the environment-scanning and analysis that policy officers or policy-minded people can do is invaluable for sensing – and making sense of – changes in the external environment.

Policy 3: Establish and maintain good links to policy and commissioning, directly or through appropriate intermediary organisations.
In some sectors and countries, it will be possible to engage positively with local and national policy makers. In Scotland, for example, the parliamentary process has been specifically designed to be collaborative and consensual. Non-profit organisations are valued because of their ability to challenge and offer solutions to decision-makers. But there and in the rest of the UK, recent changes to legislation on political lobbying have made it more difficult to engage with politicians and policy makers directly. In these and other cases, it can be useful to work with membership or umbrella bodies who represent and advocate on behalf of their sector.

This applies equally to the commissioning environment, if not more so. Some commissioners or commissioning bodies will welcome non-profit organisations providing evidence and solutions. Where this is not the case it helps to have neutral outsiders facilitating links and providing advocacy.

Again, understanding the environment in which your organisation operates is crucial for sustainability. Larger organisations will often have policy officers who can engage with policy and decision-makers, though it is getting harder to attract funding for these posts. Similarly, business development teams can develop relationships and improve mutual understanding with commissioners. Smaller organisations rely on chief officers having the capacity to make links with external stakeholders. As noted, this might mean being part of effective sector membership organisations or forming coalitions to pool resources for influencing policy and decision-making.

Policy 4: Demonstrate to policy makers and strategic commissioners how your organisation's work contributes to their work and outcomes.
Your organisation's work and its impact will only be sustainable if they matter to other people. And one of the main audiences it needs to matter to are those who are developing or funding strategies to achieve similar things.

There are various ways of achieving this, one of which is mapping your outcomes to other people's strategies and reporting on your contributions as outlined above. But a paper exercise alone is unlikely to be enough. Relationships are what will help you understand what policy makers and commissioners need, and for them to understand how your organisation can help. Again, this will be easier in some situations than in others. But what these stakeholders need most of all are evidence and ideas about affordable, effective interventions.

The more and better evidence you have, the more helpful you can be to the people who can help to sustain your impact. (This is another reason why *Policy* is part of the *Impact Measurement* capability).

Policy 5: Use evidence from evaluation and consultation to influence national and local policies and practices.

As noted, it may not be possible to exert influence on policy at all levels. But non-profit organisations have a role to play in making sure the voices of those that they represent are heard. This will be more central to some organisations' missions than others. Nevertheless, the ability to facilitate two-way links between practice and policy is a valuable tool for sustainability for the reasons outlined above. If you have gathered evidence from consultations and evaluations, it has the potential to inform not just your work, but other people's too. This can help to shape the world you – and your communities – want to be part of.

Policy 6: Be knowledgeable about your sector and well connected within it. Become known as a source of knowledge which others draw upon.

Sustainable organisations are valued parts of their ecosystem. They are not in competition with other organisations because they operate for the good of the sector and are generous with their ideas. As we have seen, they *Pioneer* new approaches by working in *Partnership*. They have effective *Profiles*, working and learning with real *Purpose*. This indicator is a reminder that sustainability is about interconnectedness, being part of and contributing to open, healthy ecosystems.

Impact Measurement: Summary

Proving

- Gather recent, relevant evidence of need, based on research and/or genuine consultation with a range of stakeholders.
- Use good quality evidence from a range of sources.
- Systematically evaluate your organisation's work and outcomes.
- Evaluation should help your organisation to learn and improve. Use it to find out what works – and what doesn't.
- Evaluation should inform future planning. Review your work before developing new services or projects.
- Communicate evaluation findings with key stakeholders (participants, partner organisations, funders etc.).

Policy

- Identify the local and national strategies your organisation's work contributes to and make reference to these in your own strategies.
- Scan the external and policy environment to identify developments in your field.
- Establish and maintain good links to policy and commissioning, directly or through appropriate intermediary organisations.
- Demonstrate to policy makers and strategic commissioners how your organisation's work contributes to their work and outcomes.
- Use evidence from evaluation and consultation to influence national and local policies and practices.
- Be knowledgeable about your sector and well connected within it. Become known as a source of knowledge which others draw upon.

We have now concluded our exploration of the Sustainability Capabilities.

Appendix 1 presents all 60 of the indicators above in a blank template to allow you to carry out a sustainability self-assessment. You can also download it as an editable PDF as part of the Lasting Difference toolkit from www.TheLastingDifference.com.

The next stage is to think about how to take action on sustainability which will require both *implementation* – and *individual leadership.*

PART 4: LEADERSHIP FOR A LASTING DIFFERENCE

The preceding chapters explored ideas and presented practical suggestions to help you plan for and take action on sustainability. They are designed to be used flexibly and I encourage you to find your own ways to do so. Sustainability has no right or easy answers. Even the sixty indicators above have been designed to support different interpretations and to lead to different answers in different organisations. In other words, there are some core elements of sustainability, but when it comes to implementation, each organisation will differ in how it chooses to prioritise and take action on them.

Nevertheless, some key learning has emerged from the way people have used the indicators and implemented the Capabilities in their organisations to date. This will be explored in this part of the book under two chapter headings.

Individual Leadership
It will not always be the chief officer of an organisation who is the first to realise that something needs to be done about sustainability. A finance officer might see it in the accounts, a frontline worker might experience it in the conflicting demands that are made on their time. Anyone in an organisation might read this book and have good ideas about how to address sustainability. So, whether you have positional authority as a manager or not, you can be a leader, contributing ideas and uniting people in action.

To help you prepare for introducing this book's ideas to your organisation, we will explore *personal priorities* and *power.* Being clear on your own aims and sources of influence will help you to lead your organisation through sustainability processes or challenges, whatever your role.

Implementation

The ideas in this book are hopefully interesting and valuable. But they are worthless if they don't help you to do something about sustainability. We will introduce some practical steps you can take to improve your organisation's chances of implementing a successful sustainability plan.

CHAPTER 16: INDIVIDUAL LEADERSHIP

Provocation: You are part of the system you are trying to change.

The world doesn't need another definition of, or book on, leadership. But for the sake of clarity, here's what I mean when I talk about leadership. It is a *process* of *influencing* and *being influenced* by *people* and *issues*, to achieve a *purpose*.

Over time, definitions of leadership have evolved. At first, the focus was on identifying the character traits of effective leaders. A little like the myth of the creative genius, this pervasive way of thinking presents some people as natural leaders. Usually, high profile, 'charismatic', powerful people (typically men) are presented as the model that others should follow. Of course, this is nonsense. We can be effective leaders without possessing any of these traits (and traits alone won't make us good leaders). So, the idea of leadership behaviours that can be learned and styles that can be adopted came to the fore. But the style that works in one situation or organisation won't work in another. So good leadership is now understood to be contingent on context and situation.

In terms of sustainability, leadership is not about creating followers, it is about equipping others with the abilities and opportunities to exercise initiative and agency. Tom Peters hits the nail on the head when he suggests that *"Leaders don't create followers, they create more leaders."*

Revisiting the Paradoxes

We began our exploration of sustainability by identifying the paradoxes that make it difficult to achieve. The same paradoxes can apply to sustainable leaders – and leadership.

The Change Paradox: Only by changing can we stay the same.
A leader needs to be able to both see changes in the external environment and help other people understand what they might mean. It is likely that some people in the organisation will be more attuned to the wider context in which they work, and more concerned about sustainability than others. They need to be able to explain these concerns to colleagues in ways they will understand, without causing unnecessary panic. Talking about sustainability can arouse fears about threats to the organisation's survival. It can also be perceived as a criticism of the organisation or the established ways of doing things.

Sustainability leaders therefore need to act as motivators and enablers, particularly during times of change. By demonstrating comfort with uncertainty and acceptance of change, leaders can help others to do the same.

Everyone can help to create a constructive environment where current thinking and practices can be challenged. Model the behaviours that you want to see in others, for example acknowledge uncertainty, ask questions, ask for and respond to feedback.

The Octopus Paradox: We need to reach out in new directions to grow. But growing in too many directions pulls us out of shape.
Effective leaders don't need to know at the outset which opportunities are worth pursuing. But they do need to understand that they can't pursue them all at once, so

they need to trust their own and other people's intuition about attractive opportunities. Being willing to test ideas and experiment with different approaches are healthy responses to the Paradox. But in order not to get pulled out of shape, leaders also need to know when to let go of things.

This in turn means being able to manage expectations, helping other people to understand that new strategies and developments are tentative, provisional. Initiatives might fail, and leaders need to be prepared to let them go if they do. People need to be given space to pursue ideas without being held to account when they don't succeed. Remember that in a changing world the riskiest strategy is not to take risks. As long as you fail fast and learn from the attempt, you have not failed.

The Yes/No Paradox: The things that we need to survive can also kill us. Saying 'yes' to everything is fatal.
This Paradox is about balancing your needs and ambitions with your capacity. It's a bit like sugar and salt. We need these to survive. They give us energy and make things taste better. But if we consume too much of them, we become ill.

We will all have different needs and ambitions at work, but we all have finite capacity. We can't do everything. Ensuring you get enough of the things you need without taking too much on is an ongoing balancing act. See *Priorities* below for ideas on finding your balance.

The Efficiency Paradox: Efficiency preserves resources but can impair development.
With limited time and resources, you need to work efficiently. But this isn't the same as working so hard that you get caught up in reactive operational issues. Or that you should feel guilty for taking time away from routine tasks to reflect on what you are doing and where you are going. It's like Steven Covey's story about the walker who sees two woodcutters struggling to chop down a tree. When asked why they don't stop to sharpen the saw, the woodcutters reply, '*We don't have time to sharpen the saw*'. Sustainable leadership requires leaders to make and protect time for proactive, strategic thinking, reflecting on their practice and sharing learning with others.

As with the organisational chicken and egg response to the Paradox, it also means having spare capacity so that leaders can build capacity. Leading sustainably means considering succession planning, building people's capacity to step up or step in. (Please note, by 'succession planning' I don't mean earmarking specific people for development or promotion opportunities, rather a capacity-building approach to ensuring leadership exists throughout the team or organisation). This is particularly important for readers who need to lead their organisation through a sustainability challenge. The people who do this most effectively always involve other people. This reduces the reliance (and pressure) on one person and helps to maintain energy and momentum.

The Myth of Perpetual Motion: The belief that work can continue without replenishing inputs.

This continues the themes about the importance of looking after yourself and other people, replenishing energy and enthusiasm for the work ahead. But it's also a reminder that, like any other change initiative, leading an organisation through a sustainability challenge requires ongoing impetus. These suggestions can help:

- Form a sustainability working group, e.g. a board sub-committee or a forum made up of people from across the organisation.
- Take time to prepare everyone who is going to be involved. Do they have the skills and resources needed to go forward?
- Use the indicators within the Sustainability Capabilities to develop action plans. Agree responsibility for leading these and monitoring progress.
- Set clear timescales, with checkpoints along the way giving everyone a chance to reflect on progress.
- Build in time for learning – individual or team development needs might emerge during the process.
- Communicate the results of the action plans regularly.
- Keep a sense of urgency and involvement. If the organisation is facing an immediate challenge or crisis, be honest about the situation and what needs to happen. Remind people of the organisation's vision and mission, and the purpose of taking action on sustainability. Make sure people and values remain at the centre of every action and conversation. Providing certainty about the things that will be sustained, even while other things are changing, can help overcome anxiety or resistance to change.

Individual leadership: Priorities

The first and most effective thing you can do to help take a lead on sustainability (or indeed, anything else) in your organisation is to identify your own personal aims and priorities for doing so. These will be different to the sustainability goals your organisation develops. Those will be quite broad and about sustaining the organisation or its impact, whereas your personal goals will be about how you relate to the situation as an individual.

What exactly do you want to achieve?

Be specific about this. Your own thoughts and feelings are part of the equation, so it is important to acknowledge them to yourself if not other people. Be clear on what you are thinking and feeling about sustainability. For instance, these are some of the personal goals that leaders I have worked with have identified:

- 'I want to not have to carry the stress of sustaining the organisation on my own anymore.'
- 'I want to enthuse other people about sustainability, but I'm worried about scaring them.'
- 'I need my manager to realise that our approach to fundraising has turned us into an octopus and it's not sustainable.'
- 'Having led the organisation through a difficult restructure I don't have the will to continue here much longer. But I want to help get the organisation back on its feet before I leave.'
- 'I want colleagues to take a more strategic approach to internal and external relationships.'

Once you have framed your goal clearly, you can begin to address it. The next step is to think about your role in bringing it about.

What needs to be done? Is this the same as what *you* need to do?
Non-profit staff and managers are motivated by making a difference. So if they see an unmet need, they might think it is their job to meet it. But when it comes to leading an organisation through a sustainability challenge, no one person can do it all themselves. There might be some goals you can achieve but there might be others you need to let go of – or seek help with.

Being clear on your personal aims helps you to work out how you want to contribute. Being clear on your role helps you to make the task manageable and seek help in the right places.

- Should you start by focusing on your own service or project rather than the whole organisation?
- Should you invite people to come together and facilitate the process, or should you lead it?
- Do you need permission for any of this?
- Who can help?

Individual leadership: Personal power

Having identified your own priorities, aims and role in exploring sustainability, it will be useful to assess your strengths and sources of influence. This is because leading a sustainability challenge is not easy. You will need to influence other people and enlist their support. You might have to overcome resistance from others. To do any of these things you will need courage, persistence and self-awareness.

- What are you good at?
- What are you recognised for within the team or organisation?

- Where will you need help from others to implement your sustainability plans?
- Who are your allies?
- What support do you need to achieve the sustainability goals you are working towards? Who is best able to give you this?

These questions apply regardless of your position within the organisation. Everyone has limitations on their ability to influence situations. Even positional authority is of limited value – chief officers can't do everything themselves, nor can they make other people do things (at least, not if they want them done well). But you might have more power than you think.

You have personal power 'over' 'in' and 'to'. You might have power 'over' people or resources, but this is of questionable value in non-profit cultures. You also have power 'in' yourself – in your character, motivation, confidence, communication skills and so on. You have the power 'to' do things, for example you might be able to contribute (or withhold) information, expertise, effort, resources and access to other people, teams or networks. And it is the ability to bring other people along that will be the biggest single determinant of the success of any sustainability plan, something we explore in the next chapter.

CHAPTER 17: IMPLEMENTATION

Provocation: If you want to go fast, go alone. If you want to go far, go together.

Organisations and leaders who have successfully used the ideas in this book report that it is essential to involve other people in the process of implementing them.

Often one or two people in an organisation will lead and co-ordinate action on sustainability. Focused attention like this can be useful when things need to be done quickly, for example if a funding deadline is approaching. But when long-term sustainability is the goal, taking the time and creating processes to involve and excite others about sustainability is vital.

Everyone in an organisation has a contribution to make to sustainability and it is important that board and staff teams are as fully engaged as possible. Harnessing the experience, energy and expertise of your colleagues will greatly increase sustainable success. It's particularly important to involve other people when completing the sustainability self-assessment in Appendix 1, as everyone will have different viewpoints - and no-one will have all the answers. But it's also useful to involve people throughout the implementation process.

Implementation: Processes

You might begin by doing your own sustainability self-assessment using the indicators in Part 3 (and Appendix 1). This will help you to identify broadly what the priorities are and who else needs to be involved - there may be indicators that ask questions you don't know the answer to, or only have a partial view on. Who has the skills or insight to help you? Who else might share your view of the situation – or be prepared to challenge it?

Create the space and time for people to do their own self-assessments and discuss the results. This works really well as part of everyday team or board meetings, or during a specially planned away day. You might want to look at the whole self-assessment or just select a few elements or indicators.

I would encourage you to share the self-assessment with everyone beforehand to give them time to think. Managers often prefer just to give people the self-assessment on the day. This is because they want the chance to explain sustainability and make sure people understand the ideas and the context without feeling daunted. Either way, the aim at this stage is to learn from each other's views, agree priorities, and identify how everyone can contribute to sustainability action plans. You might also want to seek trustworthy advice on your plans from internal or external stakeholders, especially if they have a potential stake or role in them.

Organisations and teams that use this process typically come out of it with a draft sustainability plan. But it's also very common for new strategic plans to be developed based on the sustainability assessment. Income generation strategies are another popular output. I have also known organisations to develop new involvement strategies, workplans, and appraisal processes, depending on the priorities identified.

Whatever the output, the self-assessment and action plan should identify and address the organisation's key sustainability challenges. It should be noted that the priority may not be to address weaknesses. With limited time and resources, and depending on the challenge, it may be more valuable to identify strengths and work out how to capitalise on these. If you are facilitating the process, this is one of the main things to help people to think about.

Implementation: People power

Once an action plan has been made, it is ideal if involvement is preserved and ownership continues to be shared.

- You might identify sustainability champions who are supported to co-ordinate activity across the organisation.
- Boards might create a sustainability sub-committee, making the most of Board and team members' expertise and experience.
- Staff might form new working groups or develop action plans within their existing teams.
- Beneficiaries, communities and external stakeholders might also have a useful role, for example beneficiaries might want to campaign or tell other people about the value of your work; funders might be able to introduce you to other funders.

PART 5: EXIT STRATEGIES

CHAPTER 18: SUSTAINABLE IMPACT

The idea of sustainable impact has been threaded throughout this book. Although we have identified that nothing is self-sustaining, a lasting difference can be made in three ways and at different levels: individual and community; organisational; policy and population. The ways different organisations go about this, and the emphasis they place on the three levels, will vary greatly. However, some common approaches will be evident, and these are summarised below.

Encouraging individual and community independence and ownership
The best way to make a lasting difference is to help ensure that the people – or issues – you support need you less in future.

Full independence isn't always possible or desirable. Interdependence is a more natural human and organisational state. For example, Disabled people in the Independent Living Movement describe independence as having the support they need to live the lives they want to live. Organisations can make a sustainable impact by recognising people's and communities' strengths and abilities and supporting agency and self-reliance.

Sustainable impact comes when people have opportunities to identify their own goals, work towards them, reflect on progress and plan next steps. This is why *Involvement* and *Impact Measurement* matter, and why the most powerful sustainability question is *'Who does your work belong to?'*.

The more that non-profit organisations believe that issues, challenges, opportunities and solutions belong to them, the less sustainable they and their impact will be. Some non-profit organisations talk about wanting to do themselves out of a job by fulfilling their mission, but in reality, they are reliant on people's reliance on them.

Reflection:
How close is your organisation to making this rhetoric a reality?
And how comfortable are you with your answer to that question?

Developing organisational learning and capacity
Two of the biggest risks to sustainability are unchecked growth and mission drift. Organisations need to be sufficiently focused and responsible to accept that some issues or projects are not their core business. Sometimes there are more appropriate organisations to take a project forward. Where there aren't, organisations still need to think carefully before filling the void.

One of the most helpful ways organisations can make a lasting difference is to improve other organisations' understanding of, and commitment to, their work, issues or client groups. For some organisations, improving other services' policy and practice is an important goal in its own right. This might be done directly, by providing information, resources or training to other organisations, or indirectly by raising awareness, publicising issues or campaigning. It can even happen quite subtly by modelling good practice. For example:

- A group of autism support organisations realised that taking children with autism to community leisure facilities made the children more familiar with the staff and service – and vice versa. Over time, the organisations didn't need to provide so much one-to-one support, as leisure facilities had become better able to welcome and support autistic children.

- Towards the end of a five-year government programme to tackle sectarianism, many organisations decided to wind-down their funded projects. Some had integrated anti-sectarianism into their broader work on equalities. Others had generated learning about how to engage communities with the topic or produced resources that others could use for doing the same. They had also collected these in online and physical archives. Some organisations simply realised they were not the most suitable agencies to carry the work forward. Others had supported volunteer and community-led groups to lead the issue for themselves.

In recent years, the trend has been for non-profit organisations to be funded or commissioned not just for the activities carried out, or even the outcomes achieved, but for the learning that is generated. Your funding application may be measured by how well you can contribute to other organisations' learning about what works.

Even when things end, learning can help to build a bridge to the future. Indeed, sharing and preserving learning are sometimes the only way to ensure a lasting difference. For example, projects or models that wind up (e.g. due to lack of funding) can be more easily resurrected if key learning has been preserved. Preserving learning within your organisation is also helpful, as it can help to evidence the need for future work and the effectiveness of the approaches that have been tried.

Increasing influence on policy and populations

In the same way that some organisations will encourage their work to be adopted or mainstreamed by others, some will aim to have their messages accepted by policy makers or whole populations.

This might be at a local, national or international level. It will often be the result of working in coalition with other non-profit organisations and agencies, or with their large memberships where they have them, to exert maximum influence. It's therefore not always possible to measure or attribute success. Nevertheless, one of the key measures of success is whether key messages, language and asks have been used in public or political discourse. For instance, policy and advocacy organisations often monitor (directly or via a media monitoring service) the number and nature of mentions their issue gets in parliamentary debate. Others aim to influence political parties' manifestos ahead of elections, or to inform policy as it gets developed. The belief is that if messages can be adopted in these ways, they will be embedded in public laws or policies, and therefore stand a chance of making a lasting difference at a population level.

Many of these organisations will also run campaigns aimed directly at the general population. The challenge with this from a sustainability perspective is whether messages should focus on generating support for the campaign message or for the organisation behind it. High profile publicity campaigns are expensive and resource-intensive, so it is understandable that organisations might want them to have a dual purpose. Generating campaign support helps to make a sustainable difference, so organisations may altruistically accept that issues are bigger than them – and don't belong to them. On the other hand, generating organisational support helps increase *Involvement* and *Income Generation*, both of which are appealing. However, it is rare to find examples of organisations doing both well. So, when planning campaigns, organisations first need to be clear:

- Who are they trying to reach?
- What are they trying to change? Awareness? Behaviour?
- What are they trying to increase? Support for the organisation? The issue? Or both?
- What is the best way to make a lasting difference?

This is like the dinner party metaphor we used when exploring *Profile*: who is coming to dinner (market)? What do they like to eat (message)? How shall we serve it (medium)?

CHAPTER 19: APPROACHING THE EXIT

Sustainability is not about keeping things the way they are or preserving the status quo. It means accepting change and recognising that things end. The tricky thing can be knowing when and what to change.

In any lifecycle, including organisations and services, there are periods of growth and decline. The time to take action on sustainability is when things are going well. Charles Handy calls this the 'second curve' – being ready to start a new period of growth before decline sets in. In reality, organisations don't usually take action early enough, until things have reached crisis point – until it's too late. When it comes to taking action on sustainability, timing is very important, particularly for projects, which are time-limited by definition. It's never too early to start doing something about sustainability. See below for some quick ideas to help projects prepare using the five Capabilities. Because project lengths vary, but their length is usually known from the outset, actions are listed under broad headings based on milestones and lifecycle stages rather than periods of time.

At the start of a project – Conception

> **Involvement:** Get to work on your Involvement Strategy. Enlist stakeholders' support and encourage ownership by consulting on project design, outcomes and approaches.

Income generation: Create an Income Generation Strategy. Begin identifying potential partners and funders by understanding your current ones. What value do you add for them?

Innovation: Agree what innovation means for your organisation. What role does the project have in generating new ideas and learning? How will they be received and used by the organisation?

Improvement: Start thinking ahead to the second curve of development. How else could the work develop? What other models of delivery could be used? Remember, sustainability means change not stasis.

Impact measurement: Create a monitoring and evaluation plan. Set up systems to measure relevant information, including outcomes.

A third of the way through a project - Gestation

Involvement: Review your approach to involvement to make sure it is inclusive and accommodates different people's preferences.

Income generation: Implement your Income Generation Strategy. Remember that retaining existing relationships and sources of income is easier and more cost-effective than finding new ones. Reflect this in the time and attention you spend on each.

Innovation: Identify the innovations and learning that have emerged so far. Have developments already been incorporated into your work, or do plans need to be adapted?

Improvement: Take time to reflect on what can be learned from your work to date. Adapt and change your project if things aren't going to plan. Most funders welcome this, so don't be afraid to share your ideas with them and other supporters.

Impact measurement: Check your evaluation processes to make sure they're effectively gathering the information you will need later.

At the halfway stage - Development

Involvement: This is the perfect time to involve stakeholders in planning for the future of the project. Create a sense of urgency and ownership – Who does the project 'belong' to? Who would feel its loss? What do you need from each other?

Income generation: How is the work evaluating? If it is successful, there are good reasons for it to continue. Start identifying funding and relationships that could help sustain the work into future years.

Innovation: Generate or collate learning and ideas that have been developed. Before considering new ideas for the future, screen them against your current aims, values, capacity and strategy.

Improvement: Use evaluation and feedback to improve internal processes. Start attending or organising events to share your learning and influence practice.

Impact measurement: Collate and analyse the information you have collected about activity and outcomes. Draw conclusions – what does the information tell you about how the project should proceed? Also, plan ahead for final evaluation – are there any evidence gaps to fill between now and then?

Two-thirds of the way through a project - Maturity

Involvement: Engage stakeholders' support for the future of your work. Use the exit strategy summary in Chapter 20 to identify the most appropriate model to pursue in the weeks and months ahead.

Income generation: Initiate discussions with key partners about the future (funders, commissioners etc.) and continue identifying and approaching other sources of income.

Innovation: Work with others to share innovations throughout your organisation. Identify new opportunities and directions the work could take.

Improvement: Identify recommendations for how the project could be improved in future. This is invaluable for evidencing the need for future work.

Impact measurement: Analyse information and create an in-house evaluation report. This makes reporting to other people easier and less time-consuming.

Three-quarters of the way through a project - Decline

Involvement: Work towards the exit strategy you have identified, taking care to involve stakeholders (particularly beneficiaries, staff and volunteers). How can any adverse impacts of your exit strategy be minimised and the benefits maximised?

Income generation: Finalise arrangements for future funding. If this has not already been done and the work is to continue, urgent action is needed. Contingency plans should also be made. Based on different financial scenarios, which elements of the project will be wound down, preserved or transferred?

Innovation: Make decisions about new opportunities or directions. If exiting the work, make sure learning is recorded.

Improvement: Share learning. This is likely to be why people funded or supported the work. Having evidence of learning can also help make the case for future funding.

Impact measurement: Produce final reports, identify and disseminate learning. What has been achieved? What difference has been made? What types of intervention were more effective? Did any new or unmet needs emerge? Were there any unintended outcomes, negative or positive?

CHAPTER 20: EXIT STRATEGIES

We might think of exit strategies as being the opposite of sustainability. But the Change Paradox requires us to accept that things change, and things end. In particular, projects should be thought of as time-limited pieces of work with a definite end date.

This chapter sets out the most common exit strategies and summarises their implications. The strategies are particularly relevant for projects but may also be necessary for organisations facing sustainability and survival challenges.

Mainstreaming

In this model, the organisation recognises a project's value by mainstreaming the project in the main body of the organisation. The project's staff, work and ideas are adopted as new core elements of the organisation. Any residual project funding may be brought back into the organisation. Alternatively, new resources may be invested (e.g. reserves or unrestricted income) to further development of the initiative.

Mainstreaming therefore requires strategic and potentially financial investment. It has the advantage of providing continuity of service and staffing, allowing the organisation to retain key knowledge – and stakeholder relationships.

Adoption

In this model, the project's value is still recognised, but it is absorbed into the work of another team or post within the organisation. The project's work will still continue but may have to compete with other priorities the team or postholder have. This will most likely result in less development work taking place, but that may be quite appropriate. For instance, the project may have generated all the learning it can, or its operating procedures may be well enough established that they no longer need to be piloted.

However, if project staff are not retained (and they may not be), knowledge – and key stakeholder relationships – could be lost. It is important that appropriate handover takes place so that learning is shared. Stakeholders will also need to be assured about continuity and contingency plans, particularly any funders who still have a stake in the work.

Re-funding

This is the default exit strategy in many organisations, but it should not be viewed as an easy option to avoid making difficult decisions about project continuation or closure.

In this model, ongoing funding is sought for the project, but this should only take place once the organisation has reviewed the need for, and anticipated effectiveness of, continuation. It is also important to ensure the project is still aligned to other strategic aims and priorities. Because of this, and the equally important need to align with the aims and priorities of a new funder, the project's scale and scope may change. This continual development, based on re-identification of need and realignment with internal or external priorities may be a healthy source of regeneration for the organisation. But where it is required because there is not enough resource or support for what should really be a mainstreamed service (not a time limited project), sustainability problems will recur with each cycle of re-funding.

Reconstitution

Reconstitution typically happens when a project or group starts to take on a new purpose or direction from its original intention, or when it needs more attentive development than the organisation can give it. The organisation may therefore support the project to constitute itself as a separate entity (for example as a community or volunteer-led group or as a social enterprise).

A common example of this is when organisations host user-led support groups which subsequently develop significant capacity, autonomy or resources. Such groups often reach the point that they need to move beyond the confines of the organisation to grow or achieve their own goals.

As a new and separately constituted body, the project may be eligible for different funding. The Myth of Perpetual Motion is important here. Organisations seeking to reconstitute one of their projects need to remember that the new entity will still need support and resources, including funding for salaries of any project staff who have been transferred to the new entity.

Transferal

In some ways this strategy is the opposite of mainstreaming. The project's value has been demonstrated, but it is not seen as core to the organisation. When this happens, projects (or their models or activities) may be transferred from the original organisation to a new one.

For example, a national park authority set up an outdoor activity project to encourage people to use and benefit from its land. But long-term, the authority took the decision to transfer the project because it was not contributing to the authority's core purpose of preserving the landscape. The authority identified a partner in the health sector which could provide a better fit for the project. The partner organisations then worked together to arrange for a smooth transfer, ensuring continuity of staffing and retaining the goodwill of project beneficiaries and funders.

Legacy materials

This final model recognises that the project will end, so it focuses on producing materials that can help to preserve project learning or outputs. For example, a youth education project was wound up at the end of the funding period following the successful production of a resource toolkit. An online repository was found for the toolkit, hosted by a partner organisation, which meant the project's legacy and learning were retained.

The Myth of Perpetual Motion is again relevant here. Resources may still be needed after the project ends. For example, materials may need to be reviewed and updated periodically, web hosting fees may apply, or new print runs may be required. Similarly, the sustained impact of the work will be limited. Legacy materials can raise awareness of topics but do not provide practical opportunities to address them. Having said that, preserving learning in this way does allow a project to be resurrected as and when further needs (or funding) arise. For example, an employability project needed to be mothballed for a year to allow further evidence to be gathered and funding to be put in place. An evaluation report from the first project phase was used to capture and distil key learning that could be drawn on when the project was resurrected at a later stage.

Preserving learning

You will have noticed that each of these strategies has a common element – learning. Whether it is mainstreamed, adopted, or transferred, preserving learning is the key to any successful exit strategy. If you need to work towards an exit strategy, try to identify where the learning is, where it belongs (and who to) and how it can best be preserved.

It is not always possible to sustain projects, or organisations, or even their impact. But as long as there is learning there is always hope of a lasting difference being made.

APPENDIX: RESOURCES

This appendix contains two resources:

- A sustainability self-assessment template
- An exit strategy planning template

Both are available as writable PDFs within the free Lasting Difference Toolkit, available from www.TheLastingDifference.com

Appendix 1: Sustainability self-assessment template

The self-assessment encourages you to assign a score to each indicator, using this suggested scoring guide:

2 = We have good evidence of this
1 = Evidence is mixed or patchy
0 = We cannot evidence this

You don't need to complete the self-assessment in one sitting, and you will almost certainly find it easier and more beneficial if you do it alongside other people. It's not a box-ticking exercise: it's a powerful tool for reflection and planning. Whether doing it alone or with others, look out for the most relevant indicators – the ones that make you think or that make you feel uncomfortable. Make notes and comments, as these will often be more meaningful than a score and will help inform discussion. Once you have finished the assessment, make an action plan to address the main findings. Remember that with limited time, energy and resources, it will be important to identify strengths to build on, not just weaknesses to address.

Involvement: Participation

1. We are clear on who we want to reach with our work (e.g. numbers, demographics, location).
2. We identify the needs and aspirations of our stakeholders and the people we work with – and change our services in response to these.
3. We understand the types and levels of involvement people want to have with us and have a range of appropriate opportunities for them to do so.
4. We involve people in exploring different ways to run or sustain the service.
5. We are clear on the outcomes and benefits of involvement, for our organisation and the people we work with.
6. We prioritise accessibility and equality. Other than our eligibility criteria there are no barriers to full participation.

Involvement: Partnership

1. We have good, up to date knowledge of other organisations, their priorities and what we can achieve by working together.
2. We do things with our people and partners, not to them.
3. Our staff, volunteers, participants and stakeholders are partners in our success. They are involved in the things we do and the decisions we make.
4. We encourage partners and communities to share ownership of our work, e.g. identifying which parts of projects they could support, make referrals to, fund or deliver.
5. Our systems and ways of working tie in with other organisations', where appropriate.
6. Our partners describe us as effective. Collaboration helps us harness resources and achieve things we couldn't do alone.

Income Generation: Pounds and Pence

1. We have an effective, holistic Income Generation Strategy that aligns marketing, communication, stakeholder engagement and fundraising.
2. We identify and review our projects' true costs and make sure these are covered by funding. When this is not the case it is for clearly-expressed strategic reasons.
3. We receive funding from an appropriate range of sources.
4. We are clear on the value we can add to funders without being led by their requirements.
5. We actively track when funding for projects or posts is due to end and put plans in place to review or renew it. Staff and trustees are involved in this.
6. We identify and take action on financially-failing projects.

Income Generation: Profile

1. Our approach to raising our profile is consistent with our core purpose and the impact we want to make for our communities.
2. We have identified our existing and potential markets.
3. We promote the organisation and its projects with clear messages, to clearly identified audiences, using appropriate methods.
4. We measure the effectiveness and cost-effectiveness of the promotional and income generation work we do.
5. Colleagues at all levels (e.g. managers, staff, trustees) are clear on their role in promoting the organisation.
6. We have identified advocates (e.g. participants, partners, referrers) who help to promote our work and reach new audiences.

Innovation: People

1. People are committed to the organisation's vision, culture and ethos.
2. We encourage the development of innovation, ideas and inspiration among our people, e.g. using team away days, training people in creative thinking and sharing learning.
3. We allocate time and resources to allow everyone to contribute ideas for innovation and improvement.
4. We encourage collaborative and networking activities which support problem solving, idea generation and celebrating success.
5. Staff and volunteers are supported to develop within and beyond their current roles, e.g. job shadowing, mentoring, attending conferences.
6. Leaders act as change agents, challenging team members to critically explore and frame problems and encouraging innovative solutions.

Innovation: Pioneering

1. Our organisational culture encourages and supports innovation. Experimentation, risk and failure are valued, within safe limits.
2. We actively support organisational and service development (e.g. via pilots, short-term projects, learning exchange). We capture the learning and exploit the opportunities that emerge.
3. We work with other organisations to innovate new approaches to common challenges.
4. Information and innovations are shared effectively between staff, management and trustees.
5. Our problem solving and decision-making processes allow us to carefully consider the available evidence, weigh up the options and involve the right people.
6. We are a learning organisation using everyone's knowledge and skills to produce solutions to challenges.

Improvement: Purpose

1. The organisation and its projects are united by a shared vision and identity that everyone understands (e.g. projects use organisational systems; services use organisational branding).
2. We embody our values, and embed learning and reflection, in our everyday practice, at all levels of the organisation.
3. Our culture supports and encourages teamwork, participation, empowerment, creative problem solving and idea generation.
4. Our organisation defines success based on the development of our people and the people and communities we serve.
5. We navigate and manage external pressures (e.g. money, societal changes, stakeholders) to make sure we work within capacity without compromising our values.
6. We recognise when capacity is overstretched and take action to balance demand and capacity so that quality, safety and staff wellbeing are not compromised.

Improvement: Planning

1. We work to achieve and sustain results that meet or exceed the needs and expectations of our customers, staff and stakeholders.
2. We systematically measure and improve the quality of our work.
3. We strike a good balance between planning and responsiveness. Our strategic and operational plans set parameters but leave room for creativity and emergence.
4. Our board and/or committees are diverse, well established, and have the right skills and experience to guide our work. Their make-up and effectiveness are regularly reviewed.
5. We take a holistic approach to risk management and identify and respond to opportunities and threats effectively.
6. We continue to review and refine our approach, including services, staffing and structures.

Impact Measurement: Proving

1. We have recent, relevant evidence of need, based on research and/ or genuine consultation with a range of stakeholders.
2. We use good quality evidence to support impact measurement. We gather information from a range of sources, including practitioners, beneficiaries, third parties and others.
3. We systematically evaluate our work and outcomes (the difference we make).
4. Evaluation helps us to learn and improve. We are interested in finding out what works – and what doesn't.
5. Evaluation informs future planning. We review our work before developing new services or projects.
6. We communicate evaluation findings with key stakeholders (participants, partner organisations, funders etc.).

Impact Measurement: Policy

1. We identify the local and national strategies our work contributes to and refer to these in our own strategies.
2. We actively scan the external and policy environment to identify developments in our field.
3. We have good links to policy and commissioning, directly or through appropriate intermediary organisations.
4. We demonstrate to policy makers and strategic commissioners how our work contributes to their work and outcomes.
5. We use evidence from our consultations and evaluations to influence national and local policies and practices.
6. We are knowledgeable about our sector and well connected within it. We are seen as a source of knowledge which others draw upon.

Appendix 2: Exit strategy template

Use this tool at the start or end of a piece of work, for planning and communicating how you will fulfil your obligations to stakeholders. Who could affect or be affected by your organisation's potential exit from a project and how will you manage this?

Intended model for continuing or exiting your project:					
Desired outcome:					
Stakeholder	**How are they involved in or affected by the exit strategy?**	**What actions are needed to manage this?**	**Who will do this?**	**When by?**	**Progress/ review**
Participants					
Staff					
Volunteers					
Funders					
Project partners					
Referral agencies					
Other stakeholders					

REFERENCES

This book is informed by 30 years of experience, training and study. It draws on a wide array of approaches including complexity theory, systems thinking, design thinking, realistic evaluation and relationship marketing. Chapter by chapter references and recommended reading are provided below. While I have made every effort to cite all of my influences, if you think I have omitted or not credited a source please let me know and I will put this right in future editions. Weblinks were accessed between June 2018 to March 2019.

Contact:
info@wrenandgreyhound.co.uk
@WrenGreyhound

Chapter 1 Introduction

In 2015/16 there were 166,001 voluntary organisations in the UK, more than in 2014/15 (165,801) but slightly fewer than in 2013/14 (166,334).
https://data.ncvo.org.uk/a/almanac18/finance-overview-2015-16/

The number of US non-profits registered with the Internal Revenue Service increased by 2.8 percent from 2003-2013.
https://www.urban.org/research/publication/nonprofit-sector-brief-2015-public-charities-giving-and-volunteering

The UK charity sector's income increased by £1.6bn (4%) to £47.8bn in 2015/16.
https://data.ncvo.org.uk/a/almanac18/finance-overview-2015-16/

Between 2003 and 2013, US non-profit revenues grew 30.7%
https://www.urban.org/research/publication/nonprofit-sector-brief-2015-public-charities-giving-and-volunteering

The paid workforce in the UK voluntary sector increased by 27% between 2004-2016.
https://www.ncvo.org.uk/policy-and-research/vol-sector-workforce

In the UK, the top 3% of voluntary organisations (by turnover) account for 81% of the sector's total income.
https://data.ncvo.org.uk/a/almanac18/finance-overview-2015-16/

Since 2002/3, UK Government 'voluntary' grants have fallen by around 66%, while there has been a 48% rise in 'earned' (contract) income.
https://data.ncvo.org.uk/a/almanac17/income-from-government-2/

NCVO estimates a reduction of £3.3bn in public sector funding of the voluntary sector between 2010/11–2015/16.
https://data.ncvo.org.uk/a/almanac12/how-are-public-sector-spending-cuts-affecting-the-voluntary-sector/

The public's trust in charities has fallen in Scotland and the UK
https://scvo.org.uk/policy-research/evidence-library/2018-the-public-view-trust-confidence-and-support-of-charities-in-scotland-2018

https://charitycommission.blog.gov.uk/2016/06/28/how-can-we-rebuild-public-trust-in-charities/

The Financial Health of the United States Nonprofit Sector, Morris, G. et al Oliver Wyman 2018

Nonprofit-Government Contracts and Grants: Findings from the 2013 National Survey Pettijohn, S.L. and Boris, E.T., Urban Institute 2013

Chapter 2 About non-profit sustainability

Creating Shared Value, Porter M.E. and Kramer, M.R., Harvard Business Review Jan-Feb 2011

Images of Organization, Morgan, G. Sage Publications 1997

Chapters 3-9 The paradoxes of sustainability

The Ansoff Product Market Growth Matrix https://www.ansoffmatrix.com/

For more on the interesting visual history of organisational structure charts:
https://commons.wikimedia.org/wiki/Organizational_chart

Trustee skills and effectiveness:
https://www.charitygovernancecode.org/en
https://www.oscr.org.uk/

http://goodgovernanceaward.org.uk/
https://governancecode.scot/

Understanding Organizations (4th Edition), Handy, C. Penguin 1993

The Empty Raincoat, Handy, C. BCA 1994

Strategy as Stretch and Leverage, Hamel, G. and Prahalad, C.K. in The Strategy Reader (2nd Edition), Segal-Horn, S(ed.), Blackwell 2004

Working bent over: *Flawless Consulting* (2nd Edition), Block, P. Jossey-Bass Pfeiffer, 2000

Turn off your email and phone notifications, reduce stress, increase focus and productivity: *The Organized Mind: Thinking Straight in the Age of Information Overload*, Levitin, D. Penguin, 2015

Redundancy in nature and gene duplication's role in evolution: https://en.wikipedia.org/wiki/Gene_duplication

Scotland's Sustainable Procurement Duty: http://www.legislation.gov.uk/asp/2014/12/section/9

The collapse of the outsourcing firm Carillion: https://www.civilsociety.co.uk/voices/kathy-evans-who-wants-to-be-a-carillion-heir.html and https://www.economist.com/britain/2018/01/18/where-did-carillion-go-wrong

Evidence of more organisations refusing or handing back contracts that do not cover full costs: http://www.ccpscotland.org/resources/service-provider-optimism-survey/

Scotland Funders' Forum is a good example of funders working together to harmonise their processes, particularly the work that was done on 'Harmonising Reporting' in 2008, which created a shared language and common expectations of reporting, along with standard report templates which have been adopted by many funders.

Scotland Funders' Forum makes the observation that between 5-8% of project time and budgets are spent on self-evaluation: *'Turning the Tables'*, Scotland Funders' Forum/New Philanthropy Capital, 2008.

According to the 2018 Managers and Professionals Salary Survey by the Chartered Management Institute, managers worked an extra 44 days a year over and above their contracted hours.
https://www.managers.org.uk/campaigns/salary-survey-2018

In 2019, a survey by the Association of Chief Executives of Voluntary Organisations found that chief officers work an average of 10 hours per week beyond their contracted hours, the equivalent of three months' unpaid work each year.
https://www.acevo.org.uk/news/pay-and-equalities-survey-2019-year-average-charity-ceo-will-spend-three-months-working-no-pay

Chapter 10 Involvement

Collaboration for a purpose and resources – resource dependency theory.
https://en.wikipedia.org/wiki/Resource_dependence_theory

The 7 Habits of Highly Effective People, Covey, S. Simon and Schuster, 2004

The Community Empowerment (Scotland) Act 2015
https://www.gov.scot/publications/community-empowerment-scotland-act-summary/

The importance of treating donors fairly:
https://www.theguardian.com/society/2016/jan/20/poppy-seller-who-killed-herself-got-up-to-3000-charity-mailings-a-year and https://www.institute-of-fundraising.org.uk/library/treatingdonorsfairly/

The Power of Positive Deviance, Pascale, R. et al, Harvard Business Press 2010

Organisations are more likely to do well if their partners are doing well: *Developing Relationships in Business Networks*, Hakansson, H. and Snehota, I. Routledge, 1995

Involvement taxonomies and tools:

- International Association for Public Participation https://www.iap2.org/default.aspx.
- Scottish Community Development Centre http://www.voicescotland.org.uk/.
- National Development Team for Inclusion https://www.ndti.org.uk/

Chapter 11 Why partnerships are integral to sustainability

Shadow work: https://en.wikipedia.org/wiki/Shadow_work

Chapter 12 Income Generation

'Half the money I spend on advertising is wasted; the trouble is I don't know which half.' John Wanamaker *(attributed)*

Relationship Marketing: Creating Stakeholder Value, Christopher, M. et al, Butterworth-Heinemann, 2008

Chapter 13 Innovation

The Core Competence of the Corporation, Prahalad, C.K. and Hamel, G. in The Strategy Reader (2nd Edition), Segal-Horn, S(ed.), Blackwell 2004

Creative Problem Solving: The Basic Course, Isaksen, S. G. and Treffinger, D. J. Bearly Ltd. 1985

Carl Sagan quote from Cosmos television programme: https://youtu.be/7s664NsLeFM

Adaptors and Innovators: A Description and Measure, Kirton, M. in *Journal of Applied Psychology*, 1976, Vol. 61, No. 5, 622-629. See also https://kaicentre.com/

Personal Knowledge: Towards a post-critical philosophy, Polyani, M. University of Chicago Press, 1974

On Organizational Learning (2nd Edition), Argyris, C. Blackwell, 1999

Chapter 14 Improvement

Should we all be looking for marginal gains? Matthew Syed article for BBC News https://www.bbc.co.uk/news/magazine-34247629

The What, The Why and The How of Purpose: A guide for leaders. Chartered Management Institute 2018 https://www.managers.org.uk/~/media/Files/Reports/Guide-for-Leaders-White-Paper.pdf

Contemporary Strategy Analysis (7th Edition), Grant, R.M. John Wiley and Sons 2011

Of Strategies, Deliberate and Emergent, Mintzberg, H. and Waters, J.A. in The Strategy Reader (2nd Edition), Segal-Horn, S(ed.), Blackwell 2004

Chapter 16 Individual Leadership

The bases of social power, French, J. R. P. and Raven, B. In Group dynamics, D. Cartwright and A. Zander (Eds). Harper & Row 1959

The Motivation-Hygiene Concept and Problems of Manpower, Herzberg, F. in Personnel Administrator (January–February 1964) (27): 3–7.

Chapters 18-20 Exits

The Empty Raincoat, Handy, C. BCA 1994

Independent living: http://www.ilis.co.uk/

About the author

With nearly 30 years' experience at all levels of the UK public and voluntary sectors, Graeme Reekie has been in demand as a consultant, facilitator and speaker since 2006. Based in Scotland, his company name (Wren and Greyhound) was first used in 2001 to publish Graeme's first book *Teaching Your Granny Not to Suck Eggs*. Now a creative management consultancy working specialising in supporting non-profit organisations, the company develops strategies, publishes practical tools and provides imaginative approaches to impact measurement, income generation, involvement, innovation and improvement. Graeme is particularly interested in non-profit sustainability, helping organisations to make sense of and find their way through complex challenges relating to survival and growth. Home is with a small wren and a large cat.

About Wren and Greyhound

Wren and Greyhound is a creative management consultancy run by Graeme Reekie. A five-strong team work alongside Graeme, carrying out consultancy, design and research. We help organisations to:

- **Create it:** Facilitation and coaching
  Calm, engaging facilitation of group processes and individual development.

- **Measure it:** Impact measurement
  Providing blissfully jargon-free evaluation support.

- **Plan it**: Strategy and planning
  Creative thinking for managers, teams and boards, from planning through to implementation.

- **Sustain it:** Expert consultancy
  Effective business development strategies.

Since 2006 Wren and Greyhound have helped many hundreds of organisations of all shapes and sizes. Our client list includes international, national and local charities, funders, service providers, policy and campaign groups, membership bodies and social enterprises. In an average year we work with 40 main clients and support around a 1000 more through workshops, training sessions and conferences.

You can find more of our resources at:
www.TheLastingDifference.com
www.WrenandGreyhound.co.uk

Printed in Poland
by Amazon Fulfillment
Poland Sp. z o.o., Wrocław